1

W9-AOD-029

Table of Contents

Introduction

You've arrived in the world of lean and green! You purchased this cookbook because you want to make a significant shift in your life. You may have tried other dietary habits, often very stringent ones, but you're back where you began. The lean and green process, in fact, aims to have a nutritious but revolutionary way of life that is not too difficult to keep because the recipes I will show you are simple to prepare but, more importantly, delicious. I believe that it is crucial in a diet not to lose the enjoyment of cooking. But where does it all begin?

Before we begin, it is important to consider the strategy that will be used in this diet.

First and foremost, if you have food intolerances or suffer from illnesses such as diabetes or digestive issues, you should consult your doctor. You can begin this journey if you do not have these symptoms.

To give yourself the necessary boost, keep a notebook of all the recipes you make and the outcomes you accomplish throughout the week. By recognizing the improvements, you will have great self pleasure and will be able to continue the sprint.

Another recommendation is to tell your relatives and friends about the lean and green technique. You will not be alone on this adventure this way, and you will have great times together making the recipes or tagging them on social media.

But, as is always the case, everything must begin with you; you are your own source of motivation. You've set goals for yourself and want to accomplish them. In fact, these recipes will greatly make your life easier. You will be less frustrated and have more vitality at work, at home, and in sports. Your hair and skin for example, will be much stronger. It will be as if you had a younger and better-looking body.

When it comes to sports, it is beneficial to engage in moderate exercise. If you want to join a gym, for example, seek advice from a fitness instructor before you begin, perhaps by informing him that you are planning to follow the lean and green diet.

If, on the contrary hand, you chose not to go to the gym, even a 30-minute aerobic exercise or a brisk walk a day can greatly enhance blood circulation and skeletal muscle and bone toning. It also aids in the burning of extra calories. Lastly, on a spiritual level, you will feel lighter and more energized, especially if you can go for a nice walk-in nature.

We can finally get to the soul of the lean and green world now that we've established these crucial premises.

Characteristics of the lean and green diet

The Lean and Green diet is a low-carb diet that consists of 5 to 7 ounces of lean protein and three portions of non-starchy vegetables, which are more nutritious in fiber and lower in sugar than starchy vegetables. As a result, they are low in carbohydrates and calories when compared to starchy vegetables. Up to two servings of fat can be provided. Healthy fats are essential because they enable the body to accumulate vitamins such as A, D, E, and K. They are also beneficial to the pancreas.

Now I'll give you some lean advice:
- Always choose grilled, boiled, or baked foods over fried foods.
- Eat omega-3-rich foods like salmon or sardines at least twice a week
- Enjoy vegan dishes like tofu.

In terms of greens, at the start of our journey, it is best to avoid vegetables high in carbohydrates such as potatoes, peas, maize, carrots, or Brussels sprouts to see instant results. You can eat all of the vegetables once you've managed to reach your ideal body weight. But everyone wants to know what we're going to eat. The solution is straightforward. Pretty much everything! It is not a way of eating filled with difficult-to-find and monotonous ingredients. The real question, however, is how to eat. The lean and green diet consists of two weight-loss programs and one weight maintenance plan. As a result, it is essential to reconsider how and how frequently you eat during the day.

Many people make the mistake of eating only once per day or skipping meals. So, if you have these dietary behaviors, it's time to transform them in order to live a balanced life and enjoy food more.

• The Optimal Weight 5 & 1 Plan, which contains five fuelings and one Lean and Green meal per day. As a result, you will consume six meals per day, every two to three hours during this plan.

• The Optimal Weight 4 & 2 & 1 Plan, which consists of four fuelings, two lean and green meals, and one snack per day.

• The Optimal Health 3 & 3 Plan, which consists of three fuelings and three lean and green meals per day. This maintenance program is essential for your balance and weight stability. It includes small meals every two to three hours.

We just mentioned the expression Fueling. But what is the source of the fuel? Fueling is a monitored and counted way of snacking that enables you to maintain your body active and full of energy all day long. They are specially formulated to provide you with the proper nutrient intake for your everyday activities, both at work and while exercising. In fact, it is crucial not to lose muscle strength during this path, so it is always essential to consume a lot of proteins, natural fiber, and foods that nourish your muscle tissue. And, as previously stated, a healthier life is reached by eating foods that are not necessarily bland; in fact, recipes for tasty bars, cookies, shakes, cereals, puddings, and much more will be included in the following chapters.

The advantages of the Lean and Green diet

Compared to other diet plans, lean and green is a simple and rapid to join diet. In fact, in plans 5 and 1, you will only make preparations for one meal per day. Furthermore, many snacks are intended to be enjoyed outside of the home or on the way to work. In fact, the major characteristic of many recipes is their speed. Soups, smoothies, and some snacks, for example, can be purchased directly from the Optavia webpage and delivered to your door. Other advantages discovered include an improvement in internal wellbeing. Consider how your blood pressure will improve as a result of losing weight and eating less salt and sugar. This entails a lower risk of heart disease and high blood pressure.

Recent research on a group of 303 people has demonstrated the effectiveness of this diet. People who used the 5 & 1 method lost more than 7.2 % of their weight. Having the assistance of friends or relatives is crucial from a psychological perspective. It is advantageous to find the right power even on social networks, in the diverse communities formed by Optavia and Lean and Green mentors or similar groups to exchange suggestions. Often, in these organizations, there are also coordinators or industry professionals who frequently answer the most frequently asked questions and hesitations via forums, online meetings, or periodic gatherings.

My recommendations

In this context, I'd like to offer you some advice on how to improve your path. Keep hydrated. It is essential to drink more water than you usually do, at least 64 ounces per day. Before meals, immediately begin the day with a glass of water. This will help to increase metabolic activity and make you feel less hungry throughout the day.

To follow this advice, keep track of how often you drink and set a timer to remind you of this important appointment. The impact of the agenda cannot be overstated. It allows you to record down not only your meals but also everything you consider, your achievements as well as the moments when you thought you couldn't make it but, in the end, you won and were able to move forward.

As I previously stated, it is essential to keep consistency in one's dietary habits. In fact, it is beneficial to consume food little by little, at least 15 minutes per meal. Even just a simple snack should be enjoyed slowly to allow you to reflect on the change you are making.

Sleep is another important factor that should not be overlooked. It is essential to sleep for at least 7 or 8 hours per night in order to avoid anxiety and uncontrollable hunger.

A well-balanced eating plan, such as lean and green, allows you to sleep well and stay in shape throughout the day. To sleep much better, it is also advised to consume a cup of coffee before noon. All of this will improve the quality of your night's sleep, as will staying away from smart phones right before bed. They activate our mental skills as well as our vision, thereby maintaining the mind busy. As a result, it is best to leave at least an hour before. You can post a picture of your latest recipe right before dinner and then turn everything off. A wonderful way to sleep peacefully.

Without workouts, a nutrient path would be ineffective. As stated in the introduction, if you are not trained, it is best to begin with a light exercise of 30 minutes and gradually build up to 45 minutes over the course of two weeks. All of this is always accompanied by a fitness instructor who will demonstrate the best activity for your body. In this case, you can also share your workout sessions on social media with the whole lean and green public. We suggest doing fun things with your family and loved ones in addition to going to the gym. Going for a walk after eating or going on a weekend outing benefits everyone's health. This, too, is causing movement, and it is even more wonderful when shared with loved ones. As your body slims down, you will notice a difference in clothing when you go shopping for new clothes.

Every action you take and every outcome you obtain should be documented. Treat yourself! Set deadlines for yourself, at the end of which you will publish a picture of the new you. Give yourself an article of clothing you never thought you'd wear and appreciate with your loved ones. Every outcome is never taken for granted and must be recognized.

The Optimal Weight 5 & 1 Plan

This plan enables you to achieve your ideal weight by consuming 6 small meals per day, 1 Lean and Green meal, 5 Fuelings, and one snack.

There are numerous advantages:

• Quick weight loss.
• A diverse selection of nutritious foods.
• 60 recipes that are lean and green.
• Simple snacks to prepare and keep on hand.
• It is always full.
• Recipes for losing weight.

This plan provides the ideal balance of carbs, proteins, natural fiber, and fats to assist you in losing weight while preserving muscle strength. You can also pick from a variety of fueling options in this program, such as supplements, snacks, shakes, teas, milk shakes, bars, desserts, pasta, and much more. Proteins, which are necessary for lowering desire to eat and restoring muscle tone, will be plentiful. They can be found in meat, eggs, soybeans, nuts, beans, seeds, and legumes. They have amino acids in them.

Fibers promote intestine regularity and are found primarily in whole grains, nuts, beans, and seeds.

Probiotics, also known as good bacteria, are found in all of our foods. They are beneficial to our intestine's regularity and fight infection such as gastroenteritis and stomach pain.

The calories consumed range between 800 and 1000.

Except for people under the age of 18, and pregnant or breastfeeding women, anyone can participate in this program. If you are taking certain medicines or have an illness and are undergoing treatment, you should talk to your physician first to ensure that the program is safe for you.

This menu also includes gluten-free options. Another step toward embracing more people.

The Optimal Weight 4 & 2 & 1 Plan

This program offers two Lean and Green meals, four Fuelings, and one snack. This diet includes a wide variety of foods, including fruits, dairy, and starches.

We recommend that you adhere to this program if you have the following characteristics:

• You have diabetes, including type 2.

• You are over the age of 65 and are not fit and healthy.

• You need to lose less than 15 pounds.

The portions are also limited in this plan, and they must be ingested every two or three hours. All of this is always accompanied by regular physical activity and fluid intake.

The Optimal 3 & 3 Plan

This program is essential for keeping the weight lost as a result of one of the two diet plans selected for this diet journey. It includes small meal options consumed every two to three hours, accompanied by a variety of food options. In this case, we have three Lean and Green meals as well as three Fuelings. It is the final way to maintain stability and muscle mass, but with a plentiful quantity of fruits, lean proteins, whole grains, healthy fats, and vegetables.

It is therefore recommended to always preserve the healthy eating habits gained during this eating plan. Always keep notes, drink plenty of water, and, if possible, promote physical activity because the number of calories in this plan is increased from 1200 to 2500. So don't be worried to get acquainted with and start experiment with these ingredients. You've achieved your ideal body weight, and it's time to supplement your diet with other food products that are always beneficial to our well-being.

RECIPES

Breakfast

Delicious turkey meatballs over spaghetti squash

Servings: 4
Counts: 1 Lean, 1 Healthy Fat, 3 Green, 2 Condiments
Nutrition: 330 Calories, 40g Protein, 17g Carbohydrate, 13g Fat

Ingredients:
- ½ tsp garlic powder
- 4 oz low-fat cheddar cheese
- ¼ tsp pepper
- ¼ tsp salt
- 2 tsp olive oil
- 1/4 large spaghetti squash
- 3 eggs
- 1 cup chopped scallions

Directions:
1. Begin with the spaghetti squash. Remove both the seeds and pulp by cutting them in half.
2. Place the spaghetti on a plate in the microwave and cover with 1 inch of water. Cook in the microwave for almost 15 minutes, or until the center is soft.
3. For the turkey, combine all of the flavorings in a mixing bowl and thoroughly combine with the turkey. Form the meatballs and cook in a pan with olive oil.
4. Start creating spaghetti strings with a fork, extracting the pulp from the skin.
5. Allow the squash to cool before squeezing it to remove any remaining water.
6. In a mixing bowl, combine the spaghetti squash, salt, garlic powder, eggs, scallions, and pepper.
7. Cook the seasoned squash for around 15 minutes in a pan with olive oil, until golden brown.
8. Serve warm with the meatballs and cheddar cheese.

Mexican eggs

Servings: 4
Counts: 1 Lean, 3 Green, 3 Condiments.
Nutrition: 310 Calories, 16g Fat, 15g Carbohydrate, 27g Protein.

Ingredients:
- ¾ tsp salt
- 8 eggs
- 1lb tomatoes
- 2 jalapeno peppers
- 4 cloves garlic
- ½ cup water
- 1 green bell pepper
- 1/3 mozzarella cheese
- 1 cup of fresh cilantro
- 1 jicama

Directions:
1. Wash and trim the tomatoes, peppers, and jalapenos in half.
2. Combine all of these ingredients in a saucepan with the garlic and simmer for about 10 minutes.
3. Remove all of the ingredients and set them aside to cool.
4. Peel the tomatoes and peppers and combine them, along with the garlic, in a blender.
5. Meld in the water and salt until you have a sauce.
6. Peel the jicama and cut it into 1/8-inch slices.
7. Warm the pan and add the previously made sauce. Make 8 tiny holes and place each egg in one of them.
8. Cook everything over low flame for 5 minutes, covered with a lid.
9. At last, for each plate, we added 3/4 cup of sauce and two eggs. Put 1/2 cup cheese and 1/4 cup cilantro on top. Then end up serving with the jicama wedges.

Provolone-topped eggs with turkey bacon

Servings: 4
Counts: 1 Lean, 3 Green, 1 Condiment.
Nutrition: 340 Calories, 25g Protein, 11g Carbohydrate, 22g Fat.

Ingredients:
- Cooking spray
- 12 oz baby spinach
- 2 oz of provolone
- 8 eggs
- ¼ salt and pepper
- 6 pieces of turkey bacon
- 2 cloves garlic

Directions:
1. Begin by preheating the oven to 425°F.
2. Divide the egg whites and yolks and place them in different plates.
3. Whip the whites for around 5 minutes with a mixer to make a foam.
4. In a saucepan, start making 8 mounds of egg whites and make a small hole in the middle of each using a spoon. Cook for around 5 minutes, or until golden brown.
5. Remove everything from the oven and fill each hole with an egg yolk. Cook for another 5 minutes.
6. Meanwhile, saute the garlic in a saucepan with oil until it is fragrant. Mix in the spinach. Place the eggs on top of the spinach.

Vegetable muffins

Servings: 4
Counts: 1 Lean, 3 Green, 1 Healthy Fat, 1 Condiment.
Nutrition: 290 Calories, 29g Protein, 7g Carbohydrate, 16g Fat.

Ingredients:
- 240ml liquid egg whites
- 280g chopped spinach
- 9 eggs
- 60g feta
- ¾ cup of Greek yogurt
- ¼ tsp salt
- 140g chopped mushrooms
- 300g red bell peppers

Directions:
1. Begin by preheating the oven to 375° F.
2. Whisk together the eggs, yogurt, salt, and cheese.
3. Combine with veggies.
4. Split the mixture in half and place it in two muffin cups.
5. Cook for around 25 minutes before serving.

Burger of broccoli with cheddar

Servings: 4
Counts: 1 Lean, 3 Green, ½ Condiments.
Nutrition: 290 Calories, 25g Protein, 8g Carbohydrate, 18g Fat.

Ingredients:
- ¼ cup pepper
- 1 cup almond milk
- 9 eggs
- 4 oz reduced-fat cheddar
- 6 cups small broccoli florets
- ¼ salt

Directions:
1. Begin by preheating the oven to 375°F.
2. Arrange the broccoli on a tray with two cups of water. Put in the microwave for around 4 minutes, or until the mix softens. The broccoli should then be drained in a colander to eliminate any excess water.
3. In a mixing bowl, combine the eggs, milk, and flavorings.
4. Arrange the broccoli in an oiled saucepan and garnish with the cheddar and egg mix.
5. Bake for 45 minutes, or until a golden crunchy crust forms on top.

Flavorful grilled cheese and spaghetti squash waffles

Servings: 2
Counts: 1 Lean, 3 Geen, 3 Condiments
Nutrition: 350 Calories, 27g Protein, 18g Carbohydrate, 19g Fat.

Ingredients:
- 110g fat reduced cheese
- 470g cooked spaghetti squash
- 2 eggs
- 1/8 tsp salt
- 1/3 cup grated parmesan cheese

Directions:
1. Squeeze the cooked spaghetti squash on a tidy tablecloth to remove any extra water.
2. Combine the spaghetti squash, eggs, parmesan, and salt in a mixing bowl.
3. Warm the waffle iron, then utp the mix and cook for approximately ten minutes, or until golden brown.
4. Drizzle some cheese on top of the waffle and close the waffle iron, proceeding to cook until the cheese melts. Serve immediately.

Creamy frittata with Crab and Asparagus

Servings: 4
Counts: 1 Lean, 3 Green, 2 Healthy Fats, 3 Condiments
Nutrition: 340 Calories, 50g Protein, 14g Carbohydrate, 10g Fat

Ingredients:
- ½ tsp black pepper
- 2 ½ tbsp extra virgin olive oil
- 2 tsp sweet paprika
- 1lb lump crabmeat
- 4 cups liquid egg substitute
- ¼ cup basil, chopped
- 1 tbsp finely cut chives
- 2lbs asparagus
- 1 tsp salt

Directions:
1. Split the asparagus into tiny chunks after removing the edges.
2. Preheat the oven to 375°F.
3. Saute the asparagus in a aucespan with oil until soft, then add salt, paprika, and pepper.
4. Combine the chives, basil, crab meat, and egg substitute in a mixing bowl. Whip until well combined.
5. Mix the egg and crab mixture in a saucepan with the cooked asparagus. Cook on medium heat until the eggs begin to bubble.
6. Place the frittata in the oven for almost 20 minutes, or until golden brown.

Lunch Recipes

Tasty chicken and cheese

Servings: 4
Counts: 1 Lean, 1 Healthy Fat, 3 Green, 1 Condiment
Nutrition: 380 Calories, 45g Protein, 15g Carbohydrate, 15g Fat.

Ingredients:
- 1 lb bag mini sweet peppers
- 4 tsp reduced-fat cream cheese
- ½ reduced-fat cheddar cheese
- 12 oz cooked chicken breast
- ¾ cup low fat Greek yogurt
- ½ cup chopped cilantro
- 1 cup diced tomatoes

Directions:
1. Preheat the oven to 350 degrees Fahrenheit.
2. Combine all the ingredients in a bowl, excluding the cilantro and peppers. Put them in a saucepan.
3. After cooking for around 20 minutes, serve as a side dish alongside the peppers.

Grated spaghetti squash

Servings: 2
Counts: 1 Lean, 3 Green, 3 Condiments
Nutrition: 115 Calories, 8g Protein, 10.5 g Carbohydrate, 4.8 g Healthy Fat.

Ingredients:
- 2 cloves garlic
- ¼ reduced fat parmesan cheese
- 2 ½ lb spaghetti squash
- 1 cup reduced fat cheddar cheese
- ½ tbsp thyme
- ¼ tsp salt and pepper
- 2 eggs
- ½ reduced fat Greek yogurt

Directions:
1. Preheat the oven to 400 degrees Fahrenheit.
2. Split the squash in half, then scoop out the seeds. Put it in the oven for about 30 minutes, or until a fork can be inserted without leaving a mark. Create some spaghetti strings after letting it cool.
3. Combine the ingredients in a separate bowl, except the Parmesan. Spaghetti squash will be combined with everything.
4. Transfer the mix to a skillet and sprinkle with Parmesan cheese. Cook for around 30 minutes.

Manicotti with spinach and zucchini / EGGPLANT

Servings: 4
Counts: 1 Lean, 3 Green, 1 Condiment
Nutrition: 330 Calories, 30g Protein, 17g Carbohydrate, 17g Fat.

Ingredients:
- 2 large zucchini (OR EGGPLANT)
- ¼ parmesan cheese
- 1 egg
- 1 cup frozen and thawed spinach
- 1 cup tomato sauce
- 1 ½ cups reduced fat mozzarella
- 1 ½ part skim ricotta
- 1/8 tsp salt

Directions:
1. Turn on the oven's heat at 375 F.
2. Slice the peeled zucchini into 1 to 8-inch-thick pieces.
3. Combine the spinach, ricotta, eggs, parmesan, 1/2 cup mozzarella, and nutmeg in a bowl.
4. Layer slices of zucchini on top of one another. Place a tablespoon of ricotta at the bottom of each and then wrap them up.
5. Sprinkle some Parmesan cheese and tomato sauce over the zucchini.
6. Prepare for roughly 25 minutes.

Delicious lasagna with vegetables

Servings: 4
Counts: 1 Lean, 3 Green, 3 Condiments
Nutrition: 300 Calories, 14g Carbohydrate, 18g Protein, 15g Fat.

Ingredients:
- 1/3 cup grated Parmesan cheese
- 1 egg
- ½ pound, 94% lean ground turkey
- 1 ½ cups part-skim ricotta
- 1 ½ tomato sauce
- 2 medium zucchini
- 1 large eggplant

Directions:
1. Turn on the oven's heat at 375 F.
2. Chop the zucchini into 1/4-inch-thick pieces, vertically. Rounds of eggplant, 1/4 inch thick, should be cut out horizontally.
3. Place the salt on the baking parchment paper and arrange the vegetables. Give them 15 minutes to rest.
4. Brown the meat and tomato sauce in a saucepan.
5. Combine the ricotta, a cup of mozzarella, an egg, and the Parmesan in a bowl.
6. To prepare lasagne. In a dish that can be baked, place a third of the tomato sauce at the very end. Put a single single layer of eggplant rounds on top, then a single layer of zucchini slices. Put ricotta cheese on top of them. At least twice, repeat this technique. Add some mozzarella on top. Cook for about 45 minutes and serve hot.

Healthy Salmon Salad

Servings: 4
Counts: 1 Lean, 4 Green, 3 Condiments.
Nutrition: 350 Calories, 33g Protein, 10g Carbohydrate, 20g Fat.

Ingredients:
- 1 tsb sesame seeds, toasted
- 1 cup sliced cucumber
- 2 cups lettuce
- ½ cup radishes
- 1 cup red cabbage
- 2 scallions, minced and trimmed
- ¼ lb raw boneless, skinless salmon, cut into cubes
- 1tsb sambal
- 1,035 oz seaweed sheet
- 1 tsb sesame oil
- 3 tsb soy sauce
- 1 cup cherry tomatoes
- 1 large bell pepper

Directions:
1. Combine the sesame oil, sesame seeds, sambal, soy sauce, and chives in a bowl. Cover the fresh salmon with all of these ingredients.
2. Slice the seaweed sheet into tiny chunks and add it to the bowl's side.

Fresh salmon with a salad of tomatoes and cucumbers

Servings: 4
Counts: 1 Lean, 3 Green, 3 Condiments.
Nutrition: 360 Calories, 36g Protein, 6g Carbohydrate, 21g Fat.

Ingredients:
- 4 cups sliced cucumber
- 4 slices lemon
- 1 pint cherry tomatoes
- ¼ cup fresh chopped dill
- ¼ cider vinegar
- ¼ tsp salt and pepper
- 1 ½ lbs skinless salmon

Directions:
1. Set the oven's temperature to 350° F.
2. Combine the cherry tomatoes, dill, vinegar, and cucumber in a bowl.
3. Continue to cook the salmon until it reaches a temperature of 145°F inside.
4. Add the lemon wedges to the salad you previously made and serve it with the salmon.

Mushroom Boats with taco filling

Servings: 4
Counts: 1 Lean, 3 Green, 2 Condiments.
Nutrition: 340 Calories, 33g Protein, 11g Carbohydrate, 18g Fat.

Ingredients:
- ½ tsp cumin
- 4 large portobello mushroom caps
- ½ tsp parsley
- 4 oz reduced fat cheddar cheese
- 1tsp chili powder
- 1 clove, minced garlic
- 1, 14.5 oz can diced tomatoes
- ¼ tsp salt
- ¼ tsp ground pepper
- lb 94% lean ground beef
- 2tbsp chopped onion

Directions:
1. Trim the stems off the mushrooms. Cook them for about 5 minutes after oiling them.
2. Meanwhile, sauté the beef in a skillet with the pepper, onion, and garlic. Add the tomatoes and the seasonings, and simmer for about 10 minutes more.
3. Split the ingredients into four equal amounts and place one in each mushroom boat. On top, sprinkle some cheese.

Eggplant Filled with Shrimp and Cauliflower

Servings: 4
Counts: 1 Lean, 3 Green, 2 Healthy Fat, 3 Condiments
Nutrition: 390 Calories, 52g Protein, 17g Carbohydrate, 14g Fat.

Ingredients:
- ½ tablespoon salt
- 2 ½ tablespoon extra-virgin olive oil
- ¾ pounds shrimps
- 2 cups grated cauliflower
- 3 scallions, minced and trimmed
- ½ reduced fat Greek yogurt
- 1/8 tablespoon ground black pepper
- 2 medium eggplants
- ½ cup grated Parmesan cheese

Directions:
1. Slice each eggplant into eight 1 1/2 to 3 inch rounds. To create cups with a bottom and rim that are each 1/2 inch thick, remove the eggplant's flesh.
2. After applying a 1/4 teaspoon of salt, the eggplants are partially cooked for around 20 minutes. Allow them to cool.
3. The shrimp should be salted and peppered and stir-fried in a little oil in a skillet until they turn pink.
4. In the same skillet with the residual oil, stir-fry the eggplants for about 3 minutes while adding the shredded cauliflower on top and the scallion.
5. Combine the cauliflower, shrimp, and Greek yogurt in a bowl. The eggplant cups will be filled with this mixture. Sprinkle Parmesan cheese on top.
6. Cook in the oven at 450°F for a 15 minutes and serve.

Pie Made with Cauliflower and Melted Cheese

Servings: 2

Counts: 1 Lean, 3 Green, 3 Condiments
Nutrition: 370 Calories, 10g Carbohydrate, 14g Protein, 19g Healthy Fat.

Ingredients:
- 2tsp reduced fat cream cheese
- ¼ tsp mustard
- 1 cup reduced fat cheddar cheese
- 3 cups steamed and chopped cauliflower
- ¼ tsp garlic powder
- 1 cup reduced fat Colby jack
- ¼ tsp onion powder

Directions:
1. Set the oven's temperature to 350°F.
2. Combine the cream cheese, mustard, garlic powder, and onion powder in a skillet over low heat until smooth.
3. Add the cauliflower once the cheddar cheese has fully melted. Place the remaining cheese over it.
4. Bake the entire mixture for about 25 minutes, or until the cheese is golden brown.

Shrimp and Oriental Cauliflower Rice

Servings: 4
Counts: 1 Lean, 3 Green, 3 Condiments, 2 Healthy Fat
Nutrition: 300 Calories, 11g Fat, 12g Carbohydrate, 40g Protein

Ingredients:
- 2 tbsp canola oil
- ¼ tsp each salt and pepper
- 2 scallions, minced
- 2 tsp soy sauce
- 2 garlic cloves, minced
- 4 cups riced cauliflower
- 1 ½ lb raw shrimp, peeled
- 1 cup diced bell pepper
- 1 cup chopped green beans
- 2 whole eggs
- 4 egg whites

Directions:
1. Add the eggs to a skillet with a teaspoon of oil and cook them while shaking the pan. Take them off the stove and let them to cool.
2. Add the garlic and scallions to the same skillet with the remaining oil and cook for 2 minutes.
3. Add the shrimp and cook for a further two minutes.
4. Include the bell peppers and green beans and simmer for one minute.
5. Combine the cauliflower and soy sauce.
6. Stir the cooked vegetables and shrimp into the scrambled eggs. Serve heated after dividing into 4 equal servings.

Tasty Chicken Paella

Servings: 4
Counts: 1 Lean, 1 Healthy Fat, 3 Green, 1 Condiment
Nutrition: 300 Calories, 41g Protein, 13g Carbohydrate, 10g Fat

Ingredients:
- ¼ tsp each salt and pepper
- 1 cup diced tomatoes
- 1 cup green beans, cut into ¼ inch pieces
- 2 oz seitan chorizo crumbles
- 1 scallion, minced and trimmed
- 4 cups cauliflower rice
- 1 ½ lb skinless, boneless chicken breasts, diced into bite sized pieces
- 2 garlic cloves, minced
- 4 tsp canola oil

Directions:
1. In a saucepan, warm the oil over moderate flame while browning the chicken and seitan chorizo crumbles.
2. Include the garlic and scallions, and simmer for an additional 2 minutes.
3. To make the paella, combine the tomatoes, cauliflower rice, and green beans. Cook for a another 10 minutes, then adjust with salt and pepper and serve warm.

Mouthwatering Chicken with Asparagus

Servings: 4
Counts: 1 Lean, 3 Green, 2 Condiments
Nutrition: 350 Calories, 10 Fat, 10g Carbohydrate, 32g Protein

Ingredients:
- 1 ¾ lbs bone in, skinless chicken thighs
- 2 tbsp oregano, minced
- 2lbs asparagus, trimmed
- 2 cloves garlic, minced
- ¼ tsp each salt and pepper
- 1 small lemon, juiced

Directions:
1. Set the oven's temperature to 350°F.
2. Mix and sprinkle the chicken with salt, pepper, oregano, lemon juice, and garlic in a bowl.
3. Cook the chicken for around 40 minutes, or until it reaches an interior temperature of 165°F. After that, take it out of the oven and let it cool.
4. Next, microwave the asparagus to soften it.
5. Combine the asparagus with the chicken thighs.

Risotto of Cauliflower and Asparagus with Chicken

Servings: 4
Counts: 1 Lean, 3 Green, 1 Healthy Fat, 2 Condiments
Nutrition: 320 Calories, 43g Protein, 13g Carbohydrate, 11g Fat

Ingredients:
- ¼ tsp each salt and pepper
- 2 tbsp butter, melted
- 2 pounds boneless, skinless chicken breasts
- 4 tablespoon flake nutritional yeast
- ¼ pound asparagus, chopped
- ¼ pounds grated or riced cauliflower
- ½ cup chicken stock

Directions:
1. Preheat the oven to 350°F.
2. Garnish the chicken in a baking pan with salt and pepper. Bake for 30 minutes, or until the inner temperature has reached 165°F, with the melted butter on top.
3. Next, combine the asparagus, cauliflower rice, and chicken stock in a pot and cook until soft.
4. Remove the asparagus and cauliflower risotto from the pot and stir in the nutritional yeast.
5. Plate the risotto alongside the chicken breast.

Mexican Pork Stew

Servings: 4
Counts: 1 Lean, 3 Green, 3 Condiments
Nutrition: 370 Calories, 36g Protein, 14g Carbohydrate, 19g Fat

Ingredients:
- 1 ½ lb boneless pork loin, cut into bite sized cubes
- ¼ tsp each salt and pepper
- 1 cup sliced radishes
- 1 jalapeno, seeds and membranes removed, sliced
- 4 lime wedges
- 2 scallions, chopped
- 2 serrano chiles, seeds and membranes removed, chopped
- ½ tsp Mexican oregano
- 1 lb tomatillos, chopped and trimmed
- 2 cloves garlic
- ¼ cup cilantro, chopped
- 8 large green lettuce leaves, divided

Directions:
1. In a food processor, combine scallions, garlic, tomatillos, oregano, 4 lettuce leaves, and serrano chilies until creamy.
2. Combine the tomatillo mix and the pork in a pot. If the pork is not coated by 1 inch of puree, add some water. Garnish with pepper and salt, then cover and cook for 20 minutes.
3. Cut the lettuce into tiny bits.
4. Sprinkle the cooked pork with sliced jalapeno, radishes, shredded lettuce, cilantro, and lime wedges.

Greek style Cod

Servings: 4
Counts: 1 Lean, 3 Green, 2 Healthy Fats, 3 Condiments
Nutrition: 360 Calories, 44g Protein, 16g Carbohydrate, 13g Fat

Ingredients:
- 4 scallions, chopped, white and green parts separated
- 2 ½ tsp olive oil
- ¼ tsp dried oregano
- 2 garlic cloves
- 1 cup fresh basil leaves, chopped
- 1/3 cup reduced fat crumbled feta cheese
- 2 ½ cup diced tomatoes
- 1 tsp each salt and pepper
- 1 ¾ pounds cod fillets, cut into 12 pieces, 3 per portion
- 3 small zucchinis

Directions:
1. Cook the white parts of the scallions and the oregano in a skillet with 1 tablespoon olive oil.
2. Cook for about 20 minutes over low flame with the tomatoes and oregano.
3. In the meantime, chop the zucchinis lengthwise into 1/8-inch-thick slices.
4. Put the green parts of the scallions after the tomatoes have finished cooking.
5. Preheat the oven to 425°F.
6. Line a parchment paper-covered baking sheet and place the zucchinis on top. Garnish the cod with salt, pepper, and the rest of the olive oil.
7. Arrange the cherry tomatoes and feta cheese on top of the cod.
8. Bake for about 20 minutes, or until the core temperature of the cod reaches 145°F. Garnish with basil.

Dinner Recipes

Hispanic flavored turkey

Servings: 4
Counts: 1 Lean, 3 Green, 1 Healthy Fat, 3 Condiments
Nutrition: 380 Calories, 34g Protein, 18g Carbohydrate, 20g Fat.

Ingredients:
- ¼ tsp salt
- 2 tsp ground cumin
- 2 oz reduced fat cheddar cheese
- 4 oz sliced avocado
- 1 large bell pepper, diced
- 2 tsp chili powder
- 1 can diced fire-toasted tomatoes
- 1 ¼ lb 93% lean ground turkey
- 1 tsp oil
- 1 jalapeno pepper, diced
- 2 scallions, diced
- 2 garlic cloves

Directions:
1. In a skillet, sauté the white part of the scallions for around 4 minutes while adding pepper, garlic, and salt.
2. Continue cooking everything while adding the turkey in small chunks.
3. Include the cumin, chili powder, and tomatoes. For approximately 15 minutes, cook and simmer.
4. Combine everything in a bowl and top with an ounce of avocado and a half of cheese.

Pepperoni Italian pizza

Servings: 2
Counts: 1 Lean, 3 Green, 3 Condiments
Nutrition: 390 Calories, 37g Carbohydrate, 18g Protein, 17g Healthy Fat.

Ingredients:
- ¼ cup grated Parmesan cheese
- ½ cup of tomato sauce
- 1 1/3 reduced fat mozzarella
- 2 cups riced cauliflower
- 1 egg
- ½ Italian seasoning
- 1/8 tsp salt
- 10 slices turkey pepperoni

Directions:
1. Set the oven's temperature to 425 °F.
2. Microwave the riced cauliflower for 10 minutes. Combine the parmesan, egg, 1/3 cup of mozzarella, Italian spice, and salt after allowing it to chill.
3. Use the cauliflower mixture to form a circle that is roughly 14 inch thick.
4. Bake for about 20 minutes, or until the edges are browned.
5. Place the extra mozzarella, tomato sauce, and pepperoni pieces on top.
6. Bake until the cheese has melted, approximately 10 minutes.

Seafood with vegetables

Servings: 4
Counts: 1 Lean, 3 Green, 2 Healthy Fat, 2 Condiments
Nutrition: 290 Calories, 32g Protein, 14g Carbohydrate, 12g Fat.

Ingredients:
- ½ tsp ground pepper
- 1 medium scallion trimmed and cut into 2inch pieces
- 4 cloves garlic, minced
- 2 tsp sesame oil
- 1lb peeled, raw shrimp
- ¼ tsp salt
- 2 cup red and yellow bell pepper
- 2 tsp canola oil
- 1lb raw scallops
- 3 ½ cups broccoli florets
- 2 tsp chicken bouillon

Directions:
1. Marinade the scallops and shrimp in a skillet for 10 minutes with garlic and pepper.
2. In the meantime, boil a saucepan of broccoli. Allow them to cool.
3. Simmer broccoli, bell peppers, and garlic in a skillet with one tablespoon of canola oil for about two minutes.
4. Add one tablespoon of canola oil to the same skillet and simmer the scallops and shrimp for around three minutes with the same garlic. Add the chicken bouillon and sesame oil to finish cooking.
5. Arrange the veggies in 4 equal portions and top each with 7 ounces of cooked fish. Serve alongside scallions.

Chicken with fresh and healthy Vegetables

Servings: 4
Counts: 1 Lean, 3 Green, 1 Healthy Fat, 1 Condiment.
Nutrition: 340 Calories, 43g Protein, 15g Carbohydrate, 10g Fat.

Ingredients:
- 1 ½ cups cherry tomatoes
- ½ cup green beans, cut into ¼ inch pieces
- 4 cups cauliflower rice
- ¾ libs boneless, skinless chicken breast
- 40 green pitted olives
- 1 scallion, minced
- 2 cloves garlic minced
- ¼ tsp salt and pepper

Directions:
1. Set the oven's temperature to 350°F.
2. Add salt and pepper to the chicken and adjust. Bake for about 20 minutes, or until the interior temperature has reached 165°F.
3. Cook the rest of the ingredients for around 10 minutes while you wait.
4. Cut the chicken and place cauliflower rice around it.

Traditional Korean Bibimbap

Servings: 4
Counts: 1 Lean, 1 Healthy Fat, 3 Green, 2 Condiments
Nutrition: 280 Calories, 34g Protein, 9g Carbohydrate, 12g Fat

Ingredients:
- 1lb 95% lean ground beef
- 1 tsp sesame seeds
- 2 tsp chili garlic sauce
- ½ cup chopped green onions
- 5 cups baby spinach
- 1 tsp toasted sesame oil
- 1 cup sliced cucumber
- 2 cups riced cauliflower
- 1 tsp olive oil
- ¼ tsp salt
- 4 eggs
- 1tsp soy sauce

Directions:
1. For about five minutes, cook the spinach in a tablespoon of oil over medium heat with a little sesame oil and salt.
2. Take off the spinach from the skillet and brown the ground meat there. Cook for one minute after adding the soy sauce and chili garlic sauce.
3. In the interim, microwave the riced cauliflower for about 4 minutes with a tablespoon of water.
4. Begin by adding a 1/2 cup of riced cauliflower to the meal. Place the spinach, cucumber, and ground meat on top. Garnish your bowl by stirring in the eggs, sesame seeds, and green onions.

Creamy asparagus and crabmeat omelette

Servings: 4
Counts: 1 Lean, 3 Green, 2 Healthy Fat, 3 Condiments
Nutrition: 340 Calories, 50g Protein, 14g Carbohydrate, 10g Fat

Ingredients:
- 2 ½ tbs extra vergin olive oil
- ¼ cup basil, chopped
- 1lb lump Crabmeat
- 4 cups liquid egg substitute
- 2 lbs asparagus
- ½ tbsp black pepper
- 2 tbsp sweet paprika
- ½ tbs salt
- 1tbs finely cut chives

Directions:
1. Wash the asparagus, trim off the edges, and then chop it into little pieces.
2. Set the oven's temperature to 375°F.
3. Heat the olive oil in a skillet while the asparagus cooks. Add salt, paprika, and pepper to taste.
4. Add the liquid egg substitute to a bowl with the basil, chives, and crab meat, and stir to combine.
5. Combine the crab and egg mix in the skillet with the asparagus. Cook the eggs until they boil over medium heat.
6. Bake this combination in the oven for roughly 20 minutes, or until the eggs are set and golden brown.

Salmon filet with Vegetables

Servings: 4
Counts: 1 Lean, 3 Green, 3 Condiments

Nutrition: 300 Calories, 38g Protein, 10g Carbohydrate, 12g Healthy Fat

Ingredients:
- ½ cup chopped green onions
- 4, 5 ½ oz salmon filets
- ¼ tsp red pepper flakes
- 1tsp olive oil
- 2 garlic cloves, minced
- 1, 12 oz frozen chopped spinach and patted dry
- ½ cup part skim ricotta cheese
- 1 ½ cups chopped cherry tomatoes
- ¼ tsp salt and pepper

Directions:
1. Set the oven's temperature to 350°F.
2. For about 2 minutes, in a skillet, sauté the onions in the oil. Add the garlic and continue to simmer for an additional 2 minutes. Add tomatoes, spinach, red pepper flakes, salt, and pepper. For around 3 minutes, continue to cook and stir before letting it cool for 10 minutes. Add ricotta to the mixture.
3. Top each piece of salmon with a quarter of this veggies mixture, and bake for around 15 minutes.

Spaghetti squash with Bolognese sauce

Servings: 4
Counts: 1 Lean, 3 Green, 3 Condiments
Nutrition: 320 Calories, 32g Protein, 14g Carbohydrate, 16g Fat

Ingredients:
- 1 cup water
- 2 scallions, minced and trimmed
- 1 cup diced tomatoes
- 1 ¼ lb 94% lean ground beef
- ½ cup fresh basil
- 2 tsp reduced fat Parmesan cheese
- 1 tsp paprika
- 1 medium spaghetti squash
- ½ tsp salt
- ½ tsp salt and pepper

Directions:
1. Set the oven's temperature to 400°F.
2. Extract the spaghetti squash's seeds after cutting it in half lengthwise. Fork-cut spaghetti needs to be cooked for 30 minutes with the cut side down.
3. Once the meat is done, scoop it out with a fork and put it in a basin. Mix together three cups of spaghetti squash with a quarter teaspoon of salt and the basil leaves.
4. Next, add the ground beef to a pot along with scallions, water, tomatoes, pepper, paprika, and 1/4 teaspoon salt.
5. Place this mix into a pan that has been brought to a boil and cook it for 30 minutes.
6. Toss the spaghetti squash with this ragu and some Parmesan cheese.

Exotic Chicken

Serving: 1
Counts: 1 Lean, 3 Green, 3 Condiments, 1 Healthy Fat
Nutrition: 370 Calories, 55g Protein, 16g Carbohydrate, 12g Fat

Ingredients:

- 7 oz, raw boneless, skinless chicken strips
- ½ oz pine nuts
- ½ cup raw broccoli, chopped
- ½ cup red bell pepper, chopped
- ¼ tsp garlic and herb seasoning blend
- ½ tsp onion powder
- 2tsp light time vinaigrette dressing
- ½ cup yellow bell pepper, chopped

Directions:

1. Braise the chicken strips in the vinaigrette for at least 30 minutes and ideally for one to two hours with the seasoning blend, onion powder, and vinaigrette.
2. Cook broccoli and peppers in a skillet, using a little water to prevent burning.
3. Add the chicken to the same skillet and cook it until golden brown.
4. Roast the pine nuts in the oven until they are browned.
5. Present the chicken strips with the peppers, broccoli, and pine nuts.

Mexican Fajita

Servings: 4
Counts: 1 Lean, 3 Green, 3 Condiments

Ingredients:

- 1 ¼ lb flank steak
- 1 jalapeno, sliced
- 8 cups lettuce
- ¼ cup light sour cream
- 2 scallions
- 1 tsp ground cumin
- ¼ tsp each salt and pepper
- 1 small lime, cut in half
- 1 tsp chili powder
- 1 cup diced tomatoes
- 1 bell pepper, sliced
- 1 cup cilantro, chopped

Nutrition: 290 Calories, 13g Fat, 12g Carbohydrate, 32g Protein
Directions:

1. Turn on the grill's heat.
2. Combine the cumin, salt, pepper, and chili powder in a bowl. Add this mix to the beef as seasoning.
3. Grill the steak until the inner temperature reaches 145°F. Grill it on both sides. Turn off the heat and let it cool.
4. Next, cook the lime and scallions for two minutes.
5. Trim the scallions and cut the beef thinly. Apply the lime juice to them.
6. To finish, garnish each bowl with two cups of lettuce and an equal amount of jalapenos, tomatoes, sliced bell pepper, and cilantro. For each dish, add 5 ounces of cooked beef, 1 spoonful of sour cream, and a few onions.

Pizza with cauliflower crust and chicken

Servings: 4
Counts: 1 Lean, 3 Green, 3 Condiments
Nutrition: 310 Calories, 42g Protein, 11g Carbohydrate, 12g Fat

Ingredients:
- 1 cup shredded, reduced fat mozzarella
- 4 scallions, chopped
- 1 tsp garlic powder
- 3 eggs
- ¾ tsp salt
- 2 tbsp hot sauce
- ¾ lb skinless chicken breast, shredded
- 5 cups riced cauliflower
- 3 tbsp reduced fat blue cheese crumbles

Directions:
1. Spread the cauliflower out on a parchment-lined baking sheet and roast it at 425°F for 30 minutes, or until golden brown. Take it out of the oven, then let it cool.
2. Next, combine the eggs, salt, and cauliflower in a bowl.
3. Re-bake the combined cauliflower, pressing it into a 12-inch circle. At 400°F, bake for 8 minutes.
4. Combine the remaining ingredients, excluding the mozzarella cheese, in a bowl and set aside while the crust bakes.
5. Take the combined cauliflower out of the oven and top it with 1 cup of mozzarella and the remaining ingredients. Pizza should be baked for 12 minutes at 400°F or until golden brown.
6. Dividing the pizza into eight equal pieces (2 slices per serving).

Chicken with an Asian twist

Servings: 4
Counts: 1 Lean, 3 Green, 1 Healthy Fat, 1 Condiment
Nutrition: 400 Calories, 12g Fat, 12g Carbohydrate, 59g Protein

Ingredients:
- 1 oz chopped peanuts
- 1 medium cucumber, peeled, seeds removed, halved lengthwise
- 1 large zucchini
- 2 tsp sambal
- 2 onions, trimmed and sliced
- 1 ½ lb chicken breasts, cooled and shredded
- 1 tsp canola oil
- ½ cup chopped coriander

Directions:
1. Pulverize 12 ounce of peanuts in a blender. Combine these peanuts, canola oil, and sambal thoroughly in a bowl.
2. To make zucchini strands, use a potato peeler to slice the vegetable into thin strips. T hen chunkize the cucumbers (2 cups).
3. Add shredded chicken and peanut sauce to the noodles for flavor.
4. Fill each bowl with six ounces of chicken and one cup of zucchini noodles to finish. Add 12 cup of chopped cucumber to the top and sprinkle with 2 teaspoons each of onion and coriander. Top with the remaining peanuts.

Mediterranean style chicken

Servings: 4
Counts: 1 Lean, 1 Healthy Fat, 3 Green, 3 Condiments
Nutrition: 360 Calories, 47g Protein, 15g Carbohydrate, 15g Fat

Ingredients:
- 3 tbsp balsamic vinegar
- 4 cups steamed vegetables, like zucchini noodles or broccoli
- 2 cups grape tomatoes, halved
- 2 garlic cloves, minced
- ½ cup basil leaves, cut into small pieces
- 2 cups reduced fat shredded mozzarella
- 4, (4oz) skinless, boneless chicken breast, buttered and crushed very thin
- 2 tsp olive oil
- ¼ tsp each salt and pepper

Directions:
1. Put the garlic in a skillet and heat the oil over moderate heat for 1 minute. Tomatoes, salt, and pepper should also be added. Ten minutes of cooking are accomplished with a lid. Fresh basil should be added before removing from the heat.
2. Grill the chicken breast for a few minutes on a medium-hot grill.
3. As if making a pizza, sprinkle 12 cup of the tomato mixture and 12 cup of mozzarella cheese over each chicken breast. Cook everything for around 5 minutes, or until the cheese has melted in the oven.
4. Prepare your preferred veggies as a side dish. It can be prepared in any manner, including the oven or a pan.
5. Arrange one cup of veggies as a garnish and serve the chicken breasts with cheese and tomatoes on top.

Tacos with cheddar cheese and avocado

Servings: 4
Counts: 1 Lean, 3 Green, 1 Healthy Fat, 3 Condiments
Nutrition: 330 Calories, 36g Protein, 11g Carbohydrate, 16g Fat

Ingredients:
- 8 oz reduced fat, shredded cheddar cheese
- ¼ tsp ground black pepper
- 3 oz diced avocado
- 12 oz pork tenderloin, sliced thin
- 1 tbsp taco seasoning
- 2 cups diced tomatoes
- 8 cups lettuce, chopped
- ¼ tsp salt
- 1 cup cilantro, chopped

Directions:
1. Cut the cheese into 8 pieces.
2. Switch on the oven's grill.
3. Form one part of cheese into a 6-inch circle and place it in the center of a baking sheet lined with parchment paper. On the opposite side of the parchment paper, follow the same procedure.
4. Bake the crisps for around 7 minutes.
5. Take two cans and wrap them with aluminum foil, gently pressing, to form the taco shell shape.
6. To make the taco shells, carefully lift each cheese circle and set it on top of the aluminum foil using a knife or a spatula. Keep it in place so that it will adhere nicely and harden.
7. Carry out the same process with the remaining cheese portions.
8. In the meantime, place the pork and taco seasoning in a skillet with oil. After browning, season with salt and pepper.
9. To make one serving, layer 2 taco shells with 1/4 cup cilantro, 3 ounces of pork, 2 cups of lettuce, 1 1/2 cups of tomatoes, and 3/4 ounces of avocado.

Chicken with Broccoli with Japanese flavors

Servings: 4
Counts: 1 Lean, 3 Green, 1 Healthy Fat, 3 Condiments
Nutrition: 340 Calories, 46g Protein, 13g Carbohydrate, 10g Fat

Ingredients:
- 4 cups water
- 2 tbsp sesame seeds, toasted
- 1 tsp chili oil
- 1 oz wasabi paste
- 1 ¾ lbs boneless, skinless chicken breast
- 3 cups cauliflower florets
- 3 cups broccoli florets
- 3 tbsp soy sauce

Directions:
1. Poach the chicken breast in water until it reaches the internal temperature of 165°F for about 10 minutes.
2. In the chicken broth, boil the cauliflower and the broccoli for 45 seconds each and then put them on a plate. Spread the sesame seeds on top.
3. Then, whisk wasabi, soy sauce, chili oil, and sesame and divide into four parts.
4. Cut the chicken into slices and serve with broccoli, cauliflower, and the Japanese sauce.

Mexican Meatloaf

Servings: 6
Counts: 1 Lean, 1/6 Green, 2,5 Condiments
Nutrition: 172 Calories, 6g Fat, 10g Carbohydrate, 22g Protein

Ingredients:
- ½ tsp ground cumin
- 2 cloves minced garlic
- 2 and ¼ lbs 97% lean ground beef cooked
- 4 oz diced green chili peppers
- ½ cup salsa
- ½ cup eggbeaters
- 1 cup reduced fat Colby and Monterrey jack cheese, grated
- ½ tsp salt
- 2 tsp chili powder

Directions:
1. Preheat the oven to 375°F.
2. Combine the spices, eggs, and beef in a mixing bowl. Roll the ground beef mix into a flat square on a large piece of wax paper. Garnish with green chili and cheese. Roll the wax paper to form the structure of the meatloaf.
3. Cautiously peel away the wax paper.
4. Place the meatloaf in a baking dish and top with the sauce.
5. Bake for approximately 55 minutes.
6. Top with the residual cheese and bake for another 10 minutes, or until the cheese melts.

Salmon with Asparagus

Servings: 4
Counts: 1 Lean, 3 Green, 3 Condiments
Nutrition: 380 Calories, 22g Fat, 7g Carbohydrate, 40g Protein

Ingredients:
- 1 ½ lbs asparagus, tough ends trimmed
- ½ tsp garlic powder
- 1 ½ lbs salmon
- Lemon slices
- ½ tsp salt
- 2 tsp salt free lemon pepper seasoning
- ¼ cup grated parmesan cheese

Directions:
1. Preheat the oven to 400°F.
2. Arrange the salmon on a baking sheet with parchment paper covering it. Add some salt, lemon pepper seasoning, and lemon slices.
3. Combine garlic powder and parmesan in a mixing bowl. Arrange the asparagus around the salmon and top with the parmesan and garlic powder.
4. Bake for about 20 minutes, or until the salmon is done.

Asian Chicken with Noodles

Servings: 4
Counts: 1 Lean, 3 Green, 1 Healthy Fat, 3 Condiments
Nutrition: 280 Calories, 36g Protein, 9g Carbohydrate, 11g Fat

Ingredients:
- ½ tsp salt
- 2 tbsp sesame oil
- ½ cup fresh basil leaves
- 3 cups fat free chicken broth
- 1 ¼ lbs boneless, skinless chicken breast
- 3 cups water
- ½ cup fresh coriander leaves
- 2 fresh red hot chili peppers, cut in half, membranes and seeds removed
- 3 unpeeled zucchinis cut into noodle-like strands (5 cups noodles)
- 1 cup mung bean sprouts
- ½ medium onion, slices
- 1 medium scallion, trimmed and chopped

Directions:
1. Garnish the chicken breast with salt and pepper in a big saucepan with water.
2. Bring the water to a boil, then decrease to a simmer for about 15 minutes, or until the chicken's inner temperature reaches 165°F. Take the chicken out of the water and set it aside to cool.
3. Bring the chicken broth and water to a boil in a separate pot. Pour in the noodles. Then turn off the heat.
4. Garnish the noodles with onion, mung bean sprouts, and shredded chicken.
5. Pour in the sesame oil and broth. Sprinkle with scallions, basil, coriander, and peppers, if desired.

Japanese-style beef

Servings: 4
Counts: 1 Lean, 3 Green, 3 Condiments
Nutrition: 300 Calories, 28g Protein, 11g Carbohydrate, 17g Fat

Ingredients:
- 340g lean beef, sliced
- 4 large eggs
- 1 large head cauliflower, trimmed, riced (about 6 cups) and steamed
- ½ small onion, sliced
- 800ml water
- 3 tbsp Japanese style beef rice sauce

Directions:
1. Cook the onion for two minutes in a skillet with oil. Pour in the Japanese style beef rice sauce and water. Stir for 1 minute more.
2. Cook for about 2 minutes after adding the beef. Then remove from the heat.
3. Place an egg in a microwave-safe dish and cover with water at room temperature. Cook for about 40 seconds, then cautiously remove the water.
4. Fill a deep plate halfway with cauliflower rice. After that, add the beef mixture. Put the egg on top.

5. Cut cauliflower florets and place them in a food processor to make cauliflower rice. Put it in the microwave for about 4 minutes, or until soft.

Chinese Chicken

Servings: 4
Counts: 1 Lean, 3 Green, 1 Healthy Fat, 3 Condiments
Nutrition: 330 Calories, 48g Protein, 9g Carbohydrate, 10g Fat

Ingredients:
- 2 tbsp soy sauce
- 2tbsp and 2 tsp sesame oil
- 1 garlic clove, minced
- 2 tsp peeled and minced fresh ginger root
- 2 onions, trimmed and minced, green and white parts separated
- 110g fresh mushrooms, sliced
- 1 medium red bell pepper, membranes and seeds removed, sliced
- 2 tbsp oyster sauce
- 2 medium zucchinis, cut into noodles like strands (3 cups zucchini noodles)
- 790g boneless, skinless chicken breast, sliced
- ¼ tsp ground black pepper

Directions:
1. Cook the chicken pieces in a skillet with sesame oil over low flame. Cook until the interior temperature reaches 75°F, seasoning with black pepper. Remove from the heat and set aside to cool.
2. In the meantime, combine the oyster sauce, soy sauce, and 2 tablespoon sesame oil in a mixing bowl.
3. Warm one tablespoon sesame oil in the same skillet with the ginger, garlic, and white onion pieces. Cook for approximately one minute. Cook for another 3 minutes after adding the bell pepper and mushrooms. Finally, add the zucchini noodles and continue to mix.
4. Put the chicken and the previously made sauce. Cook for 5 minutes, or until zucchini is tender.
5. Finally, sprinkle with green parts of the onions.

Traditional Shakshuka

Servings: 4
Counts: 1 Lean, 3 Green, 3 Condiments
Nutrition: 350 Calories, 27g Protein, 20g Carbohydrate, 18g Fat

Ingredients:
- 1 tsp ground cumin
- 1 tsp canola oil
- 12 large eggs
- 1 small red bell pepper, membranes and seeds removed, chopped
- 2 cloves garlic, minced
- ½ cup fresh chopped cilantro
- Pinch of cayenne pepper
- 2 oz low fat crumbled feta
- 2 scallions, minced
- 42 oz canned diced tomatoes
- ½ tsp paprika
- ¼ tsp each salt and pepper

Directions:
1. Cook garlic, scallions, and bell pepper in oil for two minutes.
2. Cook for about 5 minutes after adding the spices and tomatoes.
3. Using a teaspoon, make 12 hollows in the tomatoes. Fill each with an egg, cover with a lid, and cook for about 5 minutes, or until the egg whites are solid.
4. Turn off the heat and serve garnished with cilantro and feta. Serve immediately.

Delicious Buffalo Chicken dip with Vegan Chips

Servings: 4
Counts: 1 Lean, 1 Healthy Fat, 3 Green, 3 Condiments
Nutrition: 340 Calories, 35g Protein, 15g Carbohydrate, 14g Fat

Ingredients:
- 3 cups sliced yellow squash
- 1 tbsp olive oil
- 1 cup low fat, shredded Colby, and Monterey jack cheese
- 1 ½ cup plain, low fat Greek yogurt
- 2 tsp lemon juice
- ½ tsp each salt and pepper
- 4 light spreadable cheese wedges
- 1, 12, 5 oz can chicken breast, drained
- ½ tsp rosemary
- 3 cups sliced zucchini
- ¼ cup hot pepper sauce
- ¼ cup ranch dressing

Directions:
1. Preheat the oven to 400°F.
2. In a mixing bowl, combine the lemon juice, salt, pepper, olive oil, and rosemary.
3. Stir in the zucchini and yellow squash.
4. Arrange the zucchini and yellow squash in a single layer on a baking sheet lined with parchment paper and bake for about 25 minutes, or until crunchy.
5. To make the dip mix, combine the hot pepper sauce, the cheeses, yogurt and the ranch dressing in a food processor.
6. Once the chips are done, place the dip mix in a separate baking tray and bake for 20 minutes, or until golden brown, bubbling, and warm.

Oriental Chicken Tikka Masala

Servings: 4
Counts: 1 Lean, 3 Green, 1 Healthy Fat, 3 Condiments
Nutrition: 310 Calories, 38g Protein, 12g Carbohydrate, 13g Fat

Ingredients:
- ½ tsp salt
- ½ tsp garlic powder
- ½ tsp onion powder
- 1 ½ lbs boneless, skinless chicken thighs, cubed
- ½ cup canned coconut milk
- ¼ cup fresh cilantro, chopped
- 1 tsp grated ginger
- ¼ tsp turmeric
- 1, 14.5 oz can diced tomatoes
- 4 cups frozen riced cauliflower
- 1 tsp cumin
- ½ tsp paprika
- ¼ tsp cayenne
- 2 tsp garam masala

Directions:
1. Combine tomatoes, coconut milk, cumin, garam masala, ginger, onion powder, garlic powder, paprika, turmeric, cayenne pepper, and salt in a mixing bowl. Then, place the chicken in a pressure cooker and top with the sauce. Close the pressure valve and the lid. Cook for 20 minutes on high pressure. Allow pressure to naturally release before opening.
2. Cook the riced cauliflower in the microwave according to the package directions.
3. Split the chicken and riced cauliflower evenly among four bowls. Sprinkle with cilantro if desired.

Healthy Chicken with Kohlrabi Noodle

Servings: 4
Counts: 1 Lean, 3 Green, 1 Healthy Fat, 2 Condiments
Nutrition: 360 Calories, 42g Protein, 15g Carbohydrate, 14g Fat

Ingredients:
- 2 cups chicken broth
- ½ cup fresh basil
- 2 green onions, cut into ¼ inch rings
- 2 tbsp reduced sodium soy sauce, divided
- 4 eggs
- 2 tbsp toasted sesame seeds
- ¼ tsp red pepper flakes
- 1 ¼ lbs boneless, skinless chicken breast, cut into slices
- 1 tsp chili oil
- 2 ½ lbs kohlrabi to yield 20 oz to 6 cups noodles

Directions:
1. Place the eggs in a frying pan with some water. Bring it to a boil and then reduce to a low heat for 6 minutes. After cooking, immerse the eggs in very chilly water for 10 minutes to cool. Put the eggs in a plastic kitchen bag with 2 tablespoons soy sauce. Allow the bag to marinate for one hour.
2. Marinate the chicken slices in one tablespoon soy sauce for about 50 minutes.
3. Scrape and slice the kohlrabi with a vegetable peeler to make long noodles.
4. Bring the chicken broth to a boil in a frying pan. Then stir in the kohlrabi noodles, chicken, and red pepper flakes. Cook for about 5 minutes.
5. Stir in the scallions and basil.
6. Remove the eggs from the soy sauce-filled plastic bag and trim them in half.
7. Divide the kohlrabi noodles, chicken, and broth evenly among four soup plates. Sprinkle with sesame seeds, 14 tablespoon chili oil, and 2 half eggs per bowl.

Vegan Recipes

Tofu with savory vegetables

Servings: 4
Counts: 1 Lean, 3 Green, 3 Condiments
Nutrition: 330 Calories, 34g Protein, 20g Carbohydrate, 14g Fat

Ingredients:
- 1 tsp salt
- 2tsp balsamic vinegar
- 1tsp garlic
- 3 ½ lbs extra firm tofu
- 2tsp extra virgin olive oil
- ½ tsp pepper
- 1tsp Parmesan cheese
- 1 medium zucchini
- ¼ cup powdered peanut butter
- 1lb eggplant

Directions:
1. Set the oven's temperature to 425 °F.
2. Halve the eggplant lengthwise, then place in a skillet with 1/4 teaspoon salt on top. For around 30 minutes, roast the eggplant from the top down.
3. Next, cut the tofu into pieces that are 1/4 to 1/2 inch thick and place them in a bowl with 1/4 teaspoon each of salt and pepper. 30 minutes is approximately right for marinating.
4. Slice the zucchini into pieces about 1/4 to 1/2 inch thick. Add 1/4 teaspoon each of salt and pepper and 1 teaspoon of oil. Grill till golden brown on both sides.
5. After the eggplant has finished cooking, scoop off the flesh and add it to the blender. Add one teaspoon of oil, the garlic, the peanut butter powder, and one-fourth teaspoon of salt. Smooth purée will be the end product.
6. In a pan, sauté the tofu slices on both sides until they are browned.
7. Arrange the tofu, zucchini, and eggplant puree on a dish. Balsamic vinegar and Parmesan cheese should be added.

Mushroom flavored tofu with zucchini pappardelle

Servings: 4
Counts: 1 Lean, 3 Green, 3 Condiments
Nutrition: 290 Calories, 33g Protein, 17g Carbohydrate, 10g Fat.

Ingredients:
- 3 scallions, minced and trimmed
- ¼ cup sour cream
- ¼ cup salt and pepper
- 8oz cremini mushrooms, sliced
- 1 fresh thyme
- 3 ½ lbs extra firm tofu, sliced
- 10 oz zucchini and yellow squash
- 1 ½ cups vegetable stock
- 1 tsp soy sauce
- 2 garlic cloves, minced

Directions:
1. Chop the yellow squash and zucchini until they resemble spaghetti.
2. Sauté the mushrooms in a skillet with the thyme, scallions, garlic, tofu, stock, and soy sauce for about 10 minutes, or until they are soft.
3. Boil some water in a pot and add the zucchini pappardelle.
4. Once the tofu has finished cooking, add the sour cream. Add salt and pepper to taste.
5. Put the mushroom tofu on a layer of pappardelle with zucchini.

Oriental tempeh with vegetables

Servings: 4
Counts: 1 Lean, 3 Green, 2 Condiments
Nutrition: 310 Calories, 28g Protein, 20g Carbohydrate, 16g Fat

Ingredients:

- 1 ½ tsp soy sauce
- ½ tsp lemon juice
- ¼ cup minced scallion
- ½ tsp salt
- ½ cup diced fresh tomatoes
- 4 ½ cups diced eggplant
- ½ tsp rice vinegar
- 1 ½ cups watercress
- ½ ground black pepper
- 20oz tempeh
- 1tsp lime juice

Directions:

1. Boil some tempeh in a saucepan, then turn the heat off and let it sit in the water for around 30 minutes.
2. Combine pepper, rice vinegar, and 1/4 teaspoon salt in a marinade for the eggplant.
3. Bake the diced eggplant in a 425°F oven for about 30 minutes, or until it is golden and cooked through.
4. Once the eggplant is cooked, add scallions, tomatoes, watercress, lemon juice, and 1/4 teaspoon salt to the marinade.
5. Take the tempeh out of the water and cut it into slices that are 1/4 inch thick. Slices should be grilled in a skillet until golden brown, about 2 minutes per side.
6. Add the tempeh and lime juice and soy sauce to the eggplant mixture.

Salad with tofu noodles

Servings: 4
Counts: 1 Lean, 3 Green, 3 Condiments
Nutrition: 250 Calories, 26g Protein, 12g Carbohydrate, 11g Fat

Ingredients:

- 1tspb ginger root, trimmed and minced
- 2 cloves garlic
- 60ml water
- 400g tofu noodles
- 2tspb rice vinegar
- 5 cups sliced cucumber
- 1tsp toasted sesame seeds
- 1tsp sambal
- 2tspb soy sauce
- 2tspb peanut butter
- 1tsp sesame oil
- 4 scallions, trimmed and sliced into long and thin strips

Directions:

1. Combine the ginger, rice vinegar, peanut butter, sambal, garlic, soy sauce, water, and oil in a bowl to make the peanut sauce.
2. Combine the tofu noodles, scallions, peanut sauce, and cucumber in a separate bowl. Serve and spread over sesame seeds.

Baked vegetables with peanut sauce

Servings: 4

Counts: 1 Lean, 3 Green, 3 Condiments
Nutrition: 380 Calories, 39g Protein, 18g Carbohydrate, 18g Fat

Ingredients:
- 1 ½ cups cauliflower florets
- ½ tbsp sambal
- 3 tbsp water
- 1 ½ cups broccoli florets
- 1 ½ cups red cabbage, cut into small pieces
- 3 ½ lbs tofu sliced into ¼ - ½ inch blocks
- 2 tbsp peanut butter
- 1 bell pepper, without seeds
- ¼ tsp salt and pepper

Directions:
1. Turn on the oven's 400° F heat.
2. Arrange all the vegetables on a baking sheet that has been generously oiled, and season them with salt and pepper. They should be roasted until caramelized.
3. In an oiled pan, toast the tofu blocks till caramel brown on both sides.
4. To create the peanut sauce, combine the sambal, water, and peanut butter in a basin.
5. To assemble the dish, arrange the tofu blocks, roasted veggies, and a sprinkle of peanut sauce on a platter.

Asian flavored tofu with vegetables

Servings: 1
Counts: 1 Lean, 1 Fat, 3 Green, 3 Condiments
Nutrition: 220 Calories, 12g Protein, 37g Carbohydrate, 8g Fat

Ingredients:
- ½ cup grated cauliflower
- ½ cup cubed eggplant
- ½ cup chopped kale
- 12oz extra firm tofu
- 1tsp sesame oil
- 1tsp rice vinegar
- 2 tbsp soy sauce

Directions:
1. Start by cutting the tofu into 1-inch cubes.
2. Mix together the soy sauce and vinegar in a bowl.
3. Place the tofu and eggplant chunks to a skillet of hot sesame oil. Both must be cooked for at least 12 minutes before turning brown. Add the kale after removing them from the skillet. For 5 minutes, sauté until browned.
4. For 4 minutes, put in the microwave the cauliflower in a bowl with a little water.
5. Arrange the greens, tofu, eggplant, and cauliflower in a plate.

Tofu crumbles with cauliflower rice

Servings: 4
Counts: 1 Lean, 3 Green, 3 Condiments
Nutrition: 310 Calories, 10g Fat, 20g Carbohydrate, 34g Protein

Ingredients:
- 3 cups cauliflower rice, cooked
- 1 cup diced tomatoes
- 3- ¾ lb extra firm tofu
- 1 cup chopped cilantro
- 2 tbsp taco seasoning
- 4 cups chopped leafy lettuce

Directions:
1. Using your fingertips, crumble the tofu until it resembles minced beef.
2. Taco seasoning is used to flavor tofu.
3. Brown the ground tofu in a skillet with a teaspoon of oil.
4. Add 15 ounces of crumbled tofu, 1/4 cup cilantro, 3/4 cup cooked cauliflower rice, 1 cup lettuce, and 1/4 cup tomatoes to each serving.

Manicotti with zucchini and spinach

Servings: 4
Counts: 1 Lean, 3 Green, 1 Condiment
Nutrition: 330 Calories, 30g Protein, 17g Carbohydrate, 17g Fat

Ingredients:
- 1 cup frozen spinach
- 1 ½ vegan ricotta
- 2 large zucchini
- 1 cup tomato sauce
- Pinch nutmeg
- 1/8 tsp salt
- 1 ½ cups vegan mozzarella, divided

Directions:
1. Turn on the oven's heat at 375 F.
2. Cut zucchini into 1/8-inch-thick slices.
3. Combine the vegan ricotta, half the vegan mozzarella, the spinach, salt, and nutmeg in a bowl.
4. Line up the layers of zucchini so that they are parallel to one another. Using a spoon, place the mixture you just made at the bottom of the zucchini and wrap them up.
5. Top with the remaining mozzarella and sauce.
6. Bake for around 25 minutes.

Oriental Curry Cauliflower

Servings: 4
Counts: 3 Green, 1 Fat, 3 Condiments
Nutrition: 166 Calories, 8g Carbohydrate, 3g Protein, 15g Fat

Ingredients:
- ½ tsp salt
- ½ tsp cayenne
- 4 tsp coconut oil
- 6 cups cauliflower florets
- ¼ cup chopped cilantro
- 1 tsp garlic powder
- ½ tsp turmeric
- 1 tsp lemon juice
- 2 tsp curry powder

Directions:
1. Turn on the oven's 450°F heat.
2. Combine the coconut oil, curry powder, lemon juice, garlic powder, cayenne, turmeric, and salt in a bowl with the cauliflower.
3. Place the salted cauliflower in a sizable baking dish, and roast for 25 to 35 minutes, or until golden brown.
4. Include cilantro and then serve.

Appetizers Recipes

Lettuce boat leaves with Shrimps

Servings: 4
Counts: 1 Lean, 3 Green, 3 Condiments
Nutrition: 350 Calories, 39g Protein, 17g Carbohydrate, 15g Fat

Ingredients:
- 4 tsp olive oil
- 2 tbsp lime juice
- ¼ cup chopped cilantro
- ¼ cup chopped red onion
- 1 chopped jalapeno pepper
- ¼ cup diced green bell pepper
- 12 large lettuce leaves
- 2 pounds raw shrimp, peeled
- 1 tbsp Old Bay Blackened Seasoning
- 1 ½ cups diced tomato
- 1 cup plain, 2% Greek yogurt
- 6 oz avocado

Directions:
1. Arrange the shrimp in a skillet and dot them with Old Bay seasoning.
2. Put half of the shrimp to a pan along with two teaspoons of olive oil. 3 minutes on each side, or until pink and done. With the leftover shrimp, carry out the same steps once again.
3. To make the avocado crema, combine the avocado, Greek yogurt, and one tablespoon of lemon juice in a processor and process until creamy.
4. Saute the tomatoes, onion, cilantro, jalapeño pepper, green bell pepper, and one tablespoon of lemon juice in a skillet to make the tomato salsa.
5. To assemble the lettuce boats, cover the lettuce leaves with the shrimp, tomato salsa, and avocado.

Tiny Cheeseburger with Bacon and cheddar cheese

Servings: 4
Counts: 1 Lean, 1 Green, 3 Condiments
Nutrition: 260 Calories, 31g Protein, 5g Carbohydrate, 12g Fat

Ingredients:
- 4-6 large green leaf lettuce leaves
- ¼ cup chopped yellow onion
- 1 tbsp yellow mustard
- 1 tbsp Worcestershire sauce
- 12 cherry tomatoes, sliced in half
- 1lb lean ground beef
- 4 ultra-thin slices cheddar cheese, each cut into 6 evenly sized rectangular pieces
- 3 pieces turkey bacon, each cut into 8 evenly sized
- 1 clove garlic, minced
- ½ tb salt
- 24 dill pickle chips

Directions:
1. Set the oven's temperature to 400°F.
2. In a bowl, combine the meat, Worcestershire sauce, garlic, and salt. Create 24 meatballs from this mix, and bake them for 15 minutes on a baking sheet. Don't turn the oven off.
3. Place the cheese on top of each meatball and return them to the oven for an additional 3 minutes to allow the cheese to melt. Allow them to cool.
4. To assemble, use a toothpick to attach the cheese-covered meatball, bacon, pickle chip, lettuce, and tomato.

Chili-stuffed Nacho Boats

Servings: 4
Counts: 1 Lean, 3 Green, 1 Condiment
Nutrition: 330 Calories, 35g Protein, 21g Carbohydrate, 13g Fat

Ingredients:
- ¼ cup chopped scallions
- 24 mini bell pepper, with stem and seeds removed
- 1, 12 oz can chicken breast, drained
- ¼ cup diced jalapeno pepper
- ½ cup plain, low fat Greek yogurt
- 2 cups low fat shredded cheddar cheese, divided
- 6oz of avocado, mashed
- 1tsp chili powder

Directions:
1. Cook the diced jalapeño in a little oil in a skillet until soft.
2. In a bowl, combine the chicken, avocado, yogurt, jalapeno, half a cup of cheese, and chili powder.
3. Stuff the extra cheese and chicken mix into each bell pepper, then cook for 4 minutes, or until the cheese has dissolved.
4. Add salsa and scallions before serving

Goat cheese flavored egg muffins

Servings: 4
Counts: 1 Lean, 3 Green, 1 Condiment
Nutrition: 290 Calories, 29g Protein, 11g Carbohydrate, 15g Fat

Ingredients:
- 1 cup liquid egg whites
- 2 cups chopped cherry tomatoes
- 9 eggs
- ½ tsp salt
- 2 oz crumbled goat cheese
- 1, 10 oz package frozen, chopped kale, patted dry
- ¾ cup plain, low fat Greek yogurt

Directions:
1. Turn on the oven's heat at 375°F.
2. In a bowl, combine the eggs, goat cheese, egg whites, Greek yogurt, and salt with a whisk.
3. Include the cherry tomatoes and greens.
4. Distribute the batter among 20 to 24 slots of a medium-sized muffin pan that have been lightly oiled.
5. Bake for 25 minutes, or until a toothpick inserted in the middle of the muffins comes out clean.

Bits of cucumber and shrimp

Servings: 3
Counts: 1 Lean, 1 Green, 3 Condiments, 2 Healthy Fat

Nutrition: 165 Calories, 6g Carbohydrate, 6g Protein, 8g Fat

Ingredients:

- ¼ tsp salt
- 1 tbsp Creole seasoning
- 2 cup cucumber
- 21oz cooked shrimp
- ½ tsp cayenne
- 2tsp cilantro
- 2tsp olive oil
- 6oz avocado
- ½ cup green onions
- 2tsp lemon juice

Directions:

1. Cook the shrimp for three minutes on each side in an oiled skillet.
2. Combine all the other ingredients to make the sauce.
3. To assemble the bits, arrange the cucumbers, the avocado-based sauce, and then the shrimp on top.

Collard greens and Parmesan-stuffed meatballs

Servings: 4
Counts: 1 Lean, 3 Green, 3 Condiments
Nutrition: 310 Calories, 41g Protein, 9g Carbohydrate, 13g Fat

Ingredients:

- 1 ¼ lb 95% lean ground pork
- 1tsbp balsamic vinegar
- 1 ½ cups chicken stock
- 12 cups chopped collard greens
- 2 tbsp low fat parmesan cheese
- ½ tsp each salt and pepper
- ¼ cup hemp seeds
- 2 eggs

Directions:

1. Bring the water to a boil in a big pot and add the collard greens. For five minutes, cook. Chicken stock is added after the water is removed. For around 30 minutes, cook the collard greens in the broth.
2. To make the meatballs, combine the eggs, ground pork, salt, and pepper.
3. Include them in the simmering pot together with the collard greens.
4. Take out the meatballs and stir in the parmesan, hemp seeds, and balsamic vinegar to the mix of collard greens. for a further five minutes.
5. Arrange collard greens as a bed for the meatballs.

Sandwich with Melted Cheese

Servings: 4
Counts: 1 Lean, 3 Green, 1 Condiment
Nutrition: 340 Calories, 20g Fat, 10g Carbohydrate, 31g Protein

Ingredients:
- ¼ tsp salt
- 2 tbsp grated parmesan cheese
- 3 eggs
- 12, 1-oz reduced fat cheddar cheese slices
- 6 cups cauliflower rice

Directions:
1. Set the oven's temperature to 425 °F.
2. For 30 minutes, spread the cauliflower rice out on a baking sheet lined with parchment paper. Take out of the oven, then allow to cool.
3. Lower the temperature to 400°F.
4. Combine the cauliflower, parmesan, eggs, and salt in a bowl.
5. Cut bread into slices that are about 14 inch thick and use 1/3 cup of the cauliflower mixture.
6. For a total of 8 cauliflower "sandwiches," repeat step 6 seven times.
7. Cook them for 8 minutes at 400 °F.
8. Take them out of the oven and put three pieces of cheddar on each piece of bread. Another layer of cauliflower bread is then placed on top. For a total of 4 cheese sandwiches, repeat this step 3 times.
9. Place the sandwiches back in the oven and heat them there until the cheese is melted.

Small Meat and Mushroom Sandwiches

Servings: 4
Counts: 1 Lean, 3 Green, 3 Condiments
Nutrition: 320 Calories, 36g Protein, 8g Carbohydrate, 18g Fat

Ingredients:
- ½ salt
- ½ tsp garlic powder
- 3 plum tomatoes, sliced
- 2 cups lettuce
- 1lb 94% lean ground beef
- 12 mushrooms caps, sliced in half horizontally
- 6 slices reduced fat Swiss cheese
- 1tbsp soy sauce
- 1tbsp Worcestershire sauce
- ¼ cup diced scallions

Directions:
1. Combine the ground beef, Worcestershire sauce, scallions, soy sauce, salt, and garlic powder in a mixing bowl. 12 flat meatballs are formed.
2. Grill the beef over low heat.
3. Place the sliced mushroom caps on the grill and cook for 2 minutes per side.
4. Chop the cheese into four slices. To make sandwiches, utilize mushroom caps as buns and layer on the slice of cheese, beef, lettuce, and tomato slices.

Asian Egg Popiah

Servings: 4
Counts: 1 Lean, 3 Green, 1 Condiment
Nutrition: 360 Calories, 29g Protein, 12g Carbohydrate, 20g Fat

Ingredients:

- 1 cup lettuce
- 1 ½ cups shitake mushroom, sliced
- 8 whole eggs
- 2 cups cabbage
- 9oz, 85% lean ground pork
- ½ cup bell pepper
- 1 ½ cups turnip, grated
- 2 cloves garlic, minced
- 1 tbsp soy sauce

Directions:

1. Warm the sesame oil in a pan on a medium heat while cooking the garlic. Add the ground pork and mix well.
2. Caramelize the pork thoroughly and cut it into tiny chunks. When it's almost done, add the mushroom, shredded cabbage, turnip, bell pepper, and soy sauce. Cook for another 15 minutes on low heat.
3. Separate the eggs and whisk them until frothy. Melt butter in a 9-to-10-inch pan on a medium heat.
4. Diffuse the egg mix into the frying pan with a 1/3 cup scoop. Start making an even layer, then carefully flip them over and cook for 30 to 60 seconds more. Wraps will result from this movement.
5. Repeat with the remaining eggs three times more.
6. Make egg wraps and fill them with 14 slices of pork each.
7. To make the wraps, close the corners with your fingers firmly like a burrito.
8. Serve whole or cut in half, hot or cold.

Tilapia and Cauliflower Rice

Servings: 4
Counts: 1 Lean, 2 Healthy Fats, 3 Green, 3 Condiments
Nutrition: 350 Calories, 51g Protein, 10g Carbohydrate, 13g Fat

Ingredients:

- 2 lbs Tilapia
- 1 tsp ground cumin
- 6 cups cauliflower rice
- 1 tsp lime juice
- 1 ½ tbsp extra virgin olive oil
- ¼ cup toasted pumpkin seeds
- 1 tsp each salt and pepper
- 1 cup coarsely chopped fresh cilantro

Directions:

1. Preheat the oven to 450°F.
2. Garnish the Tilapia with lime juice.
3. Combine the pepper, salt, and cumin in a mixing bowl. Tilapia should be seasoned with this mix.
4. Cook the Tilapia for 7 minutes in the oven.
5. Sauté the cauliflower rice in a skillet with oil until soft, about 2 minutes.
6. Toss the rice with the cilantro and pumpkin seeds.
7. Take the pan off the heat and serve with the Tilapia.

Original Chicken Parmesan

Servings: 4
Counts: 1 Lean, 3 Green, 1 Healthy Fat, 3 Condiments
Nutrition: 360 Calories, 49g Protein, 16 Carbohydrate, 12 g Fat

Ingredients:

- 1 ¾ lbs boneless, skinless chicken breast
- 2 tbsp and 2 tsp large flake nutritional yeast
- 2 cloves garlic, minced
- ½ cup almond flour
- 2 scallions, chopped
- 1, 15 oz can diced tomatoes
- 2 medium zucchini, cut and sliced into noodles like strands
- ½ tsp dried oregano
- ½ tsp each salt and pepper

Directions:
1. Preheat the oven to 400°F.
2. Combine the almond flour and nutritional yeast in a mixing bowl. Garnish the chicken breast with pepper and salt before coating it in the prepared mixture.
3. Bake for 15 minutes, or until the inner temperature of the cake reaches 165°F. Take out of the oven and set aside to cool.
4. Cook for 15 minutes in a pan with the scallions, oregano, tomatoes, and garlic.
5. Heat up the zucchini noodles in a steamer basket over boiling water.
6. Serve the chicken breast with zucchini noodles on top.

Spaghetti Squash with Shrimps

Servings: 4
Counts: 1 Lean, 3 Green, 2 Healthy Fats, 3 Condiments
Nutrition: 400 Calories, 49g Protein, 18g Carbohydrate, 14g Fat

Ingredients:

- 1 clove garlic, minced
- 1 tsp lemon juice
- ¼ tsp each salt and pepper
- ¼ cup shredded Parmesan cheese
- 1 ½ tbsp olive oil
- 1 ¾ lbs cooked and peeled shrimp
- ½ tsp crushed red pepper flakes
- 1 small to medium sized spaghetti squash
- 1 cup cherry tomatoes, diced
- ½ tsp onion powder
- 1 tbsp dried parsley

Directions:
1. Halve the spaghetti squash and scoop out the seeds. Place them in a bowl with a little water and put in the microwave for about 10 minutes. When they're cool enough to handle, use a fork to scoop out the flesh into spaghetti-like strands to yield five cups.
2. Cook the garlic for one minute in a skillet with olive oil over medium high heat.
3. Cook for another 4 minutes in the same skillet with the tomatoes, lemon juice, parsley, red pepper flakes, salt, pepper, and onion powder. Then add the spaghetti squash and continue to cook until everything is well combined.
4. Remove from the skillet and top with Parmesan cheese.

Rustic pie with broccoli and cheese

Servings: 4
Counts: 1 Lean, 3 Green, 1 ½ Condiments
Nutrition: 290 Calories, 25g Protein, 8g Carbohydrate, 18g Fat

Ingredients:

- 6 cups small broccoli florets
- ¼ tsp cayenne pepper
- 9 eggs
- 4 oz shredded, reduced fat cheddar
- ¼ tsp each salt and pepper
- 1 cup almond milk

Directions:
1. Preheat the oven to 375°F.
2. Put the broccoli in the microwave in a bowl with 3 tbsp water for about 4 minutes, or until soft. Allow to cool before removing the extra water.
3. Combine the milk, eggs, and seasonings in a mixing bowl.
4. Place the broccoli in a baking tray. Add the Parmesan on top and cover with the egg mixture.
5. Bake for 45 minutes, or until the top has created a light crust.

Tasty Pork Chops with Spinach

Servings: 4
Counts: 1 Lean, 3 Green, 3 Condiments
Nutrition: 300 Calories, 28g Protein, 12g Carbohydrate, 16g Fat

Ingredients:

- 1 tbsp lemon juice
- 1 cup diced tomatoes
- 1 tbsp jerk seasoning
- 1 tsp lime juice
- 4 bones in pork chops, about 7 ounces each
- 8 oz baby spinach
- 1 cup sliced radishes
- ½ tsp ground pepper
- ½ tsp salt

Directions:
1. Garnish and soak the pork chops for about 30 minutes with salt, jerk seasoning, and lime juice.
2. Cook the pork chops for about 10 minutes at 450°F, or until the internal temperature has reached 145°F.
3. In the meantime, cook the spinach for 2 minutes in a pot with 1 tablespoon of water.
4. Toss the spinach with the tomatoes, lemon juice, radishes, pepper, and salt in a mixing bowl.
5. Take the pork chops out of the oven and serve with the spinach salad.

Chicken Fajita with salad

Servings: 2
Counts: 1 Lean, 3 Green, 1 Healthy Fat, 3 Condiments
Nutrition: 337 Calories, 16g Carbohydrate, 14g Fat, 37g Protein

Ingredients:
- 2 tsp olive oil
- 2 tsp fajita seasoning
- 1lb chicken breast, sliced into strips
- 6 romaine leaves
- Juice of a half of a lime
- 2 bell peppers, sliced into strips

Directions:
1. Preheat the oven to 400°F.
2. In a mixing bowl, combine all of the ingredients excluding the lettuce. Blend well to coat the chicken and vegetables equally with the oil and seasoning.
3. Place everything in a baking dish lined with silver foil and bake for 30 minutes.
4. Place the lettuce leaves on top of the chicken mix.

Chicken Texas with broccoli

Servings: 4
Counts: 1 Lean, 1 Healthy Fat, 3 Green, 3 Condiments
Nutrition: 290 Calories, 10g Fat, 8g Carbohydrate, 41g Protein

Ingredients:
- 2 tbsp mayo
- ¾ cup reduced fat Greek yogurt
- 4 raw boneless, skinless chicken breasts
- 6 cups broccoli florets
- 1 tbsp BBQ seasoning
- 1 tbsp homemade ranch seasoning Ranch seasoning recipe
- 2 tbsp dried parsley
- 1 tbsp onion powder
- 2 tsp salt
- 1 tbsp dried drill
- 1 tsp black pepper
- 1 tbsp dried chives

Directions:
1. Begin heating the grill.
2. Garnish the chicken with barbecue seasoning.
3. Cook the chicken for 6 minutes, or until the inner temperature reaches 165°F.
4. In a mixing bowl, mix all of the dried herbs and spices to make the homemade ranch seasoning. Then, until ready to use, store this mix in a sealed container.
5. In a separate bowl, combine the broccoli, yogurt, mayonnaise, and ranch seasoning.
6 ounces cooked chicken and 12 cup broccoli salad make up each serving.

Broccoli morsels with Cheese

Servings: 4
Counts: 1 Lean, 3 Green, 2 Condiments, 1 Healthy Fat
Nutrition: 310 Calories, 33g Protein, 12g Carbohydrate, 15g Fat

Ingredients:
- 2 tsp olive oil
- ¼ cup parmesan cheese
- 6 cups steam in bag frozen broccoli
- 4 large eggs
- ¼ tsp salt
- 1 tsp garlic powder
- 2 cups 1% cottage cheese
- ¼ cup sliced scallions
- 1 ¼ shredded, reduced fat mozzarella cheese

Directions:
1. Preheat the oven to 375°F.
2. Cook the broccoli according to the package instructions.
3. Allow them to cool. Then, place the broccoli in a food processor and pulse until finely diced. Blend broccoli with eggs, scallions, cottage cheese, mozzarella, parmesan cheese, garlic, olive oil, and salt until well combined.
4. Split the mixture evenly among 20 to 24 slots in two lightly floured muffin tins and bake for 30 minutes, or until golden brown.

Vegetarian Pizza with Chicken

Servings: 2
Counts: 1 Lean, 3 Green, 2 Condiments
Nutrition: 290 Calories, 41g Protein, 12g Carbohydrate, 10g Fat

Ingredients:
- 2 tbsp grated parmesan cheese
- ½ cup reduced fat shredded mozzarella cheese
- 1 egg
- 1 cup baby spinach
- 1 ½ cups sliced tomatoes
- 1 cup chopped green bell peppers
- ½ lb 90%-94% lean ground chicken
- ½ tsp Italian seasoning

Directions:
1. Preheat the oven to 400°F.
2. In a mixing bowl, combine the chicken, 1 egg, parmesan cheese, and Italian seasoning. Make a thin circular crust out of this mixture. Cook for about 20 minutes on a baking sheet lined with parchment paper.
3. Arrange sliced tomatoes, spinach, mozzarella, and green bell peppers on top of the chicken crust.
4. Bake for another 10 minutes, or until the cheese has melted. Serve divided into four pieces.

Soup and Salad Recipes

Turkey Meatball Soup

Servings: 4
Counts: 1 Lean, 3 Green, 3 Condiment
Nutrition: 400 Calories, 42g Protein, 15g Carbohydrate, 19g Fat

Ingredients:
- 2 scallions, trimmed and minced
- 2 cups halved cherry tomatoes
- ½ cup low fat grated parmesan cheese
- 1 ½ lbs 93% lean ground turkey
- 1 cup chopped fresh basil
- 4 cups zucchini and yellow summer squash noodles
- 2 tbsp non perell capers
- ½ tsp black pepper
- 4 cups chicken stock

Directions:
1. Combine the ground turkey, parmesan, scallions, salt, and pepper in a mixing bowl. Create 12 small meatballs from the mixture.
2. Bring the chicken stock to a boil in a large pan, then add the capers and turkey meatballs. 14 minutes in the oven.
3. Remove the meatballs from the chicken stock and divide them among four bowls. Stay warm.
4. Bring the chicken stock back to a boil in a pot, then add the squash noodles and cook for 2 minutes. Place a quarter of the squash noodles on top of the turkey meatballs in each bowl using kitchen tongs.
5. Cook for a minute over low flame with the cherry tomatoes. Add some basil leaves as well.
6. Remove the cherry tomatoes from the pot and divide them evenly among the four bowls. Serve immediately.

Fish soup and chicken

Servings: 4

Ingredients:
- 2 cups water
- 2 cups cauliflower rice
- ¼ tb each salt and pepper
- ¾ lb peeled shrimp
- 1 ½ cups chopped okra
- 1 lb boneless, chicken thighs, cut into bite sized pieces
- 2 garlic cloves, minced
- 1 tbsp canola oil
- ¼ tsp dried thyme
- ¼ tsp cayenne
- 1 small green bell pepper, seeds and membranes removed, diced
- A bay leaf
- 1 ½ cups diced tomatoes
- 2 celery ribs, diced

Counts: 1 Lean, 3 Green, 2 Condiments, 1 Healthy Fat
Nutrition: 320 Calories, 40g Protein, 15g Carbohydrate, 12g Fat
Directions:
1. Place the scallions, garlic, celery, and bell pepper to a skillet with oil.
2. Marinate for 15 minutes with the water, tomatoes, cayenne pepper, bay leaf, and thyme.
3. Put the chicken and okra and cook for another 10 minutes.
4. Add the shrimp and cauliflower and continue to cook for another 3 minutes. If the soup becomes too dry, add more water. Garnish with pepper and salt to taste. Serve immediately.

Classic Caesar salad

Servings: 4
Counts: 1 Lean, 3 Green, 3 Condiments, 1 Healthy Fat
Nutrition: 380 Calories, 57g Protein, 8g Carbohydrate, 13g Fat

Ingredients:
- 3 tsp extra virgin olive oil
- ¼ tsp ground pepper
- 1 ½ tbsp light mayonnaise
- 1 tsp lemon juice
- ¼ cup grated Parmesan cheese
- 1 cup halved cherry tomatoes
- 1 clove garlic
- 1 tsp Worchester sauce
- 1 cup chopped eggplant
- 6 cups romaine lettuce
- ¼ tsp salt
- 1tbsp grated Parmesan cheese
- ½ tsp mustard
- 1 ½ lbs grilled chicken breast, divided
- 1 cup chopped zucchini

Directions:
1. Preheat the oven to 400°F.
2. Place the zucchini and eggplant on a baking sheet lined with parchment paper and bake for 30 minutes, or until soft.
3. In a mixing bowl, combine all of the dressing ingredients.
4. Toss the roasted vegetables with the lettuce, tomatoes, parmesan cheese, and dressing. Per serving, use six ounces of grilled chicken.

Curry soup with fish and mushrooms

Servings: 4
Counts: 1 Lean, 2 Healthy Fat, 3 Green, 3 Condiments
Nutrition: 320 Calories, 11g Fat, 9g Carbohydrate, 49g Protein.

Ingredients:
- 1 cup clam juice
- 2 scallions, minced and trimmed
- 2 tbsp and 2 tsp olive oil
- 1 tbsp Madras curry powder
- 3 ½ cups button mushrooms, halved
- 1 cup diced tomatoes
- ½ cup cilantro, chopped
- 1 cup diced daikon radish
- 1 cup water
- ½ tsp salt
- 2 lbs peeled raw shrimp

Directions:
1. Sauté the mushrooms in a hot pan with oil over medium high heat for around 10 minutes.
2. Cook for another 4 minutes after adding the daikon radish and scallions.
3. Cook for 1 minute after adding the curry powder.
4. Bring the clam juice, tomatoes, water, and salt to a boil for 2 minutes.
5. Put the shrimp and start reducing to a low heat for 2 minutes, or until the shrimp turn pink.
6. Garnish the soup with cilantro.

Traditional Greek salad

Servings: 4
Counts: 1 Lean, 3 Green, 3 Condiments, 1 Healthy Fat
Nutrition: 340 Calories, 45g Protein, 9g Carbohydrate, 14g Fat

Ingredients:
- 1 cup sliced cucumber
- 1 pint cherry tomatoes, halved
- 6 cups romaine lettuce, chopped
- 1 ¾ lbs boneless, skinless chicken breast
- ¼ tsp each salt and pepper
- 10 pitted Kalamata olives
- 1/3 cup reduced fat feta cheese
- 1 ½ tbsp butter, melted
- 1 small lemon, juiced

Directions:
1. Preheat the oven to 350°F.
2. Garnish the chicken with salt, pepper, and butter.
3. Cook the chicken for almost 25 minutes, or until the temperature inside reaches 156°F. Remove it from the oven and set it aside to cool.
4. In a mixing bowl, combine the remaining ingredients to make a salad.
5. Arrange the chicken on a bed of Greek salad and serve.

Vegan burrito salad

Servings: 4
Counts: 1 Lean, 3 Green, 3 Condiments
Nutrition: 310 Calories, 10g Fat, 20g Carbohydrate, 34g Protein

Ingredients:
- 4 cups chopped leafy lettuce
- 1 cup diced tomatoes
- 1 cup fresh cilantro, chopped
- 3 ¾ lb extra firm tofu, drained
- 3 cups cauliflower rice, cooked
- 2 tbsp taco seasoning

Directions:
1. Disintegrate the tofu with your fingers until it resembles minced beef.
2. Sprinkle the taco seasoning over the tofu.
3. In a skillet with oil, caramelize the tofu granulate over medium heat.
4. Divide 1 cup lettuce, 14 cup tomatoes, 34 cup cauliflower rice, 15 ounces tofu crumbles, and 14 cup cilantro among 4 servings.

Cheeseburger and spinach flavored soup

Servings: 4
Counts: 1 Lean, 3 Green, 3 Condiments
Nutrition: 400 Calories, 44g Protein, 11g Carbohydrate, 20g Fat

Ingredients:
- ¼ tsp salt
- 7 cups baby spinach
- 3 cups low sodium chicken broth
- 4 oz reduced fat shredded cheddar cheese
- 1lb 90% lean ground beef
- ¼ tsp ground pepper
- 2 tsp Worchester sauce
- ¾ cup diced celery
- ¼ cup chopped onion
- 1, 14.5 oz can diced tomatoes
- 1 tsp dried parsley

Directions:
1. Sauté the beef in a big saucepan until it is brown. Continue to cook the celery and onion until soft. Take the pan off the heat.
2. In a separate pan, heat the tomatoes, Worcester sauce, parsley, broth, salt, and pepper. Cook for 20 minutes on low heat with a lid on.
3. Cook for another 3 minutes after adding the spinach. Put 1 ounce of cheese on top.

Fresh and healthy tuna salad

Servings: 4
Counts: 1 Lean, 3 Green, 1 Healthy Fat, 3 Condiments
Nutrition: 350 Calories, 36g Protein, 12g Carbohydrate, 16g Fat

Ingredients:
- 4 tsp extra virgin olive oil
- 6 cups mixed greens
- 2 garlic cloves, minced
- 6 hard-boiled eggs, sliced
- 2, 7 oz cans of tuna, packed in water and drained
- 2 cups string beans, steamed
- 1 cup grape tomatoes, halved
- 3 tbsp balsamic vinegar

Directions:
1. Combine the garlic, vinegar, and oil.
2. Make the salad using the mixed greens. Make it more filling by adding tomatoes, beans, egg slices, and tuna. Garnish with the oil and vinegar mixture.

Greek style soup with chicken

Servings: 4
Counts: 1 Lean, 1 Healthy Fat, 3 Green, 1 Condiment
Nutrition: 380 Calories, 45g Protein, 15g Carbohydrate, 15g Fat

Ingredients:
- 1 ½ cups celery sticks
- ½ cup chopped cilantro
- 4 tbsp reduced fat cream cheese
- 1 ½ cups reduced fat, shredded sharp cheddar cheese
- ¾ cup low fat Greek yogurt
- 1 cup diced tomatoes with green chilies
- 1, 1lb bag mini sweet peppers, halved lengthwise, stems and seeds removed
- 12 oz, shredded, cooked chicken breast

Directions:
1. Preheat the oven to 350°F.
2. Combine all of the ingredients, except for the bell peppers and cilantro, in a mixing bowl. After that, place them on a baking sheet.
3. Bake for 20 minutes, or until done. Season with mini sweet bell peppers and celery sticks and serve immediately.

Rich vegetable soup with chicken

Servings: 4
Counts: 1 Lean, 3 Green, 3 Condiments
Nutrition: 350 Calories, 14g Carbohydrate, 12g Protein, 27g Fat

Ingredients:
- 2 cups chicken broth
- 4 cups chopped cauliflower florets
- 1tsp olive oil
- 2 cloves garlic, minced
- 2 slices turkey bacon, cooked and chopped
- ¼ cup diced onion
- 1, 5.3 oz low fat, plein Greek yogurt
- 1 ½ cups reduced fat shredded cheddar cheese
- ½ cup diced celery
- 1 bay leaf
- 1 medium zucchini, chopped
- 12 oz, cooked, boneless, skinless chicken breast, diced
- ½ tsp each salt and pepper

Directions:
1. Cook the onion in a skillet with oil, then add the celery and garlic. 4 minutes in the oven. Combine the zucchini, cauliflower, bay leaf, chicken broth, salt, and pepper in a mixing bowl. Cover and bring to a boil, then decrease to a low heat and cook for 8 minutes, or until the vegetables are soft.
2. Remove the bay leaf and set aside to cool. Using a blender, combine all of the ingredients.
3. Combine with the Greek yogurt, chicken, and 1 cup of cheese. Garnish with the residual cheese and bacon pieces if desired.

Italian Minestrone

Servings: 4
Counts: 1 Lean, 3 Green, 3 Condiments
Nutrition: 300 Calories, 12g Fat, 15g Carbohydrate, 32g Protein

Ingredients:
- 2 cups shredded green cabbage
- 1 cup fresh basil
- ½ tsp ground black pepper
- 4 tsp low fat parmesan cheese
- 1 tsp salt
- 1 cup diced yellow summer squash
- 1 cup halved cherry tomatoes
- 4 cups chicken stock
- 1 cup sliced celery
- 1 ¼ lb, boneless, skinless chicken thighs

Directions:
1. Bring the chicken and stock to a boil in a big pot. Reduce the temperature to low and sauté for 45 minutes, or until the chicken is cooked. Allow the chicken thighs to cool after removing them from the broth.
2. Put the veggies and continue to simmer in the broth for 10 minutes.
3. Once the chicken has cooled, cut it into bite-sized parts.
4. Return the chicken to the skillet. Mix in the tomatoes, pepper, and basil. Serve immediately with a teaspoon of parmesan cheese per person.

Mediterranean-flavoured soup

Servings: 4
Counts: 1 Lean, 3 Green, 3 Condiments
Nutrition: 300 Calories, 27g Protein, 7g Carbohydrate, 13g Fat

Ingredients:
- 6 cups chicken broth
- ¼ cup grated Parmesan cheese
- 1 egg
- 4 cups raw spinach
- 4 cups riced cauliflower
- 1 ¼ lbs 93% lean ground beef
- ¼ tsp salt
- 1 tsp Italian seasoning

Directions:
1. Boil half of the broth in a large pot.
2. Combine half of the Parmesan cheese, the eggs, half of the Italian Seasoning, the beef, and the salt in a mixing bowl. Create small meatballs from this mix.
3. Add the meatballs to the broth and cook for 5 minutes.
4. Bring the residual broth and Italian seasoning to a boil. Put the cauliflower rice and continue cooking for another 5 minutes.
5. Cook for another 2 minutes after adding the spinach.
6. Serve the soup with the residual Parmesan cheese on top.

Curry chicken salad

Servings: 2
Counts: 1 Lean, 3 Green, 1 Healthy Fat, 3 Condiments
Nutrition: 390 Calories, 24g Protein, 31g Carbohydrate, 14g Fat

Ingredients:
- ¼ tsp salt and pepper
- ½ cup low fat plein Greek yogurt
- 2/3 oz chopped peanuts
- 1, 10 oz can of chicken breast, packed in water
- 2 tbsp parsley, chopped
- 8 large romaine lettuce leaves
- ½ cup diced celery
- 2 tsp curry powder

Directions:
1. Mix the yogurt, celery, chicken, spices, and herbs in a mixing bowl.
2. To make the wraps, top the lettuce leaves with the chicken salad. The peanuts should be spread on top.

Healthy Salad of Chicken with Vegetables

Servings: 4
Counts: 1 Lean, 1 Healthy Fat, 3 Green, 3 Condiments
Nutrition: 300 Calories, 43g Protein, 12g Carbohydrate, 10g Fat

Ingredients:
- ¼ cup pumpkin seeds
- 8 cherry tomatoes, halved
- ¼ tsp each salt and pepper
- 1 cup riced broccoli
- 1 cup riced kabocha squash
- 1 cup riced yellow summer squash
- 1 clove garlic
- ½ cup low fat plain Greek yogurt
- 1 ½ lbs boneless, skinless chicken breast
- 1 cup riced zucchini
- 4 tbsp lemon juice
- 1 cup fresh basil
- 1 cup shredded red cabbage
- 4 radishes, sliced

Directions:
1. Preheat the oven to 350°F.
2. Season the chicken with salt and pepper.
3. Bake the chicken for 12 minutes, or until the inner temperature reaches 165°F. Then, remove it from the oven and set it aside for 5 minutes to cool. Make small pieces.
4. In the meantime, steam riced kabocha squash, yellow summer squash, zucchini, and broccoli for about 5 minutes in a microwave-safe bowl.
5. Finally, make our dressing by merging the last four ingredients in a blender and blending until smooth.
6. Divide the riced veggie mixture evenly among four bowls. Combine a quarter of the chicken and one tablespoon of seeds with the same quantity of radishes, cherry tomatoes, and shredded cabbage on top.

Fueling Hacks

Bagel with Cheddar Cheese

Servings: 1
Counts: ½ Lean, 3 Condiments

Ingredients:
- 1 sachet Optavia Select Buttermilk Cheddar Herb Biscuit
- 1 slice reduced fat cheddar cheese
- 3 tbsp cold water
- 1 tsp bagel seasoning
- 1 egg

Directions:
1. Preheat the oven to 350°F.
2. Combine the water and biscuit, split it, and spread it homogenously on two donut pan slots. Add salt and pepper to taste and bake for 15 minutes, or until the sides are golden brown.
3. Finally, cook the egg in a skillet.
4. Place an egg and cheese on one bagel slice and cover with the other.

Greedy Avocado Toast

Servings: 1
Counts: 1 Fueling, 1 Healthy Fat

Ingredients:
- 1 ½ oz avocado mashed
- 1 sachet Optavia Select Buttermilk Cheddar Herb Biscuit

Directions:
1. Cook according to the guidelines on the sachet.
2. Allow to cool before spreading with mashed avocado.

Waffles topped with potatoes and melted cheese

Servings: 4
Counts: 1 Fueling, ½ Lean, 1 Condiment

Ingredients:
- ½ cup liquid egg substitute
- 2 slices turkey bacon, cooked according to package directions and chopped into small pieces
- 4 sachets Optavia Essential Roasted Garlic Creamy Smashed Potatoes
- ¼ cup chopped scallions
- ½ cup shredded, reduced fat cheddar cheese
- ½ cup almon milk

Directions:
1. Combine milk, cheese, egg substitute, and Garlic Creamy Smashed Potatoes in a mixing bowl.

2. Pour this batter into a warm, lightly oiled waffle iron. Cook for 7 minutes, or until golden brown, with the lid closed. Remove the waffle from the iron and end up serving while still warm.

Italian style Marinara Rigatoni

Servings: 1
Counts: 1 Fueling, 2 Condiments

Ingredients:
- ½ cup origan
- ¼ cup chili powder
- 1 sachet Optavia Essential Rustic Tomato Herb Penne
- 1 cup of garlic

Directions:
1. Prepare the Essential Rustic Tomato Herb Penne according to the package directions.
2. Stir in the chili powder, garlic, and origan.

Fun Colorful Frappe

Servings: 1
Counts: 1 Fueling, 3 Condiments

Ingredients:
- 1 tbsp vanilla or almond milk
- ½ cup ice
- 1 cup vanilla or almond milk
- 1 sachet Optavia Essential Creamy Vanilla Shake
- 2 tbsp pressurized whipped topping
- 1 tbsp Walden Farm Caramel Syrup
- 1 tsp espresso powder, McCormick Color from Nature Food Colors-blu, yellow and red
- 2 tbsp plain, reduced fat Greek yogurt

Directions:
1. In a food processor, mix all of the ingredients except the Greek yogurt and whipped topping until soft.
2. Mix in the same amounts of yellow and blue food coloring until the desired shade of green is obtained.
3. In a mixing bowl, combine the Greek yogurt and an equal amount of red and blue food coloring until the desired shade of purple is obtained.
4. In a separate bowl, combine a tablespoon of milk with equal parts red and blue until the desired colouration of purple is obtained.
5. To make a Frappe, put the purple Greek yogurt mix in the bottom of a plastic cup. Fill it halfway with green shake mix. Top with the purple milk mix and whipped topping.

Sweet Pumpkin Milkshake

Servings: 1
Counts: 1 Fueling, 2 Condiments

Ingredients:
- ½ cup ice
- 4 oz strong brewed coffee, chilled
- 1 sachet Optavia Essential Spiced Gingerbread
- 2 tbsp pressurized whipped topping
- 4 oz vanilla or almon milk
- 1/8 tsp pumpkin pie spice

Directions:
1. In a blender, combine all of the ingredients except the whipped topping and blend until creamy.
2. Finish with the whipped topping and serve!

Chocolate and Peanut Butter Donuts

Servings: 4
Counts: 1 Fueling, 1 Condiment, ½ Optional Snack

Ingredients:
- ¼ cup vanilla or almond milk
- 6 tbsp liquid egg substitute
- 2 Optavia Essential Golden Chocolate Chip Pancake
- 2 Optavia Essential Decadent Double Chocolate Brownie
- ¼ cup powdered peanut butter
- 3-4 tbsp vanilla or almond milk
- ½ tsp baking powder
- ½ tsp vanilla extract

Directions:
1. Preheat the oven to 350°F.
2. Combine the pancakes, milk, vanilla extract, brownies, egg substitute, and baking powder in a mixing bowl. Bake for 15 minutes, or until the mixture is set, in four slots of a donut pan. Allow it to cool before glazing.
3. Next, make the peanut butter coating. Mix the milk and powdered peanut butter in a mixing bowl until blended and creamy. Dip each donut in the glaze and sprinkle with chocolate chips.

Cream cheese and berry donut

Servings: 2
Counts: 1 Fueling, ½ Healthy Fat, 1 ½ Condiment

Ingredients:
- 1 oz light cream cheese
- ½ tsp baking powder
- 2 sachets Optavia Essential Yogurt Berry Blast Smoothie
- 2 tbsp liquid egg substitute
- 1/3 cup almond milk

Directions:
1. Preheat the oven to 350°F.
2. Combine the Yogurt Berry Blast Smoothie, baking powder, milk, and egg substitute in a mixing bowl.
3. Pour this mix into the four slots of a donut pan.
4. Cook for 15 minutes, or until the mix has firmed up. Spread the crem cheese on them once they've cooled.

Goat cheese muffins

Servings: 4 (3 muffins per serving)
Counts: 1 Fueling, ½ Lean, ½ Healthy Fat, 2 Condiments

Ingredients:
- 1 oz crumbled goat cheese
- 1 cup almond milk
- 4 sachets Optavia Honey Sweet Potatoes
- 1/8 tsp nutmeg
- 1 tbsp chopped rosemary
- ¼ cup diced yellow onion
- 4 eggs
- 2/3 cup part-skim ricotta

Directions:
1. Preheat the oven to 375°F.
2. Combine milk and Honey Sweet Potatoes in a mixing bowl. Then, microwave it for 1 12 minute on high. Allow it to cool.
3. Combine the rest of the ingredients in a mixing bowl.
4. Divide the mix evenly among the 12 muffin tin slots.
5. Bake for 30 minutes, or until the corners turn golden brown.

Biscuits with Greek yogurt and chocolate

Servings: 1
Counts: 1 Lean, 1 ½ Lean

Ingredients:
- 1 sachet Optavia Essential Chewy Chocolate Chip Cookie
- 1, 5.3 oz low fat plain Greek yogurt

Directions:
1. Incorporate the Greek yogurt and the Chewy Chocolate Chip Cookie sachet. Mix well and serve chilled.

Pizza Muffins

Servings: 4 (3 muffins per serving)
Counts: 1 Fueling, ½ Lean, ½ Healthy Fat, 2 Condiments

Ingredients:
- 2 tsp olive oil
- 1 cup basil leaves
- 4 sachets Optavia Buttermilk Cheddar Herb Biscuit
- 2 tbsp balsamic vinegar
- 4 oz fresh mozzarella, cut into 12 small pieces
- ½ cup almond milk
- 3 plum tomatoes, sliced

Directions:
1. Preheat the oven to 450°F.
2. Combine the milk, oil, and Buttermilk Cheddar Herb Biscuit in a mixing bowl.
3. Spread the mixture evenly among the 12 muffin tin slots.
4. Fill evey slot with a piece of tomato, a slice of mozzarella, and a few basil leaves.
5. Bake for 12 minutes, or until the cheese has melted and bubbly.
6. Before serving, drizzle with balsamic vinegar.

Creamy Potatoes with Spinach and Cheese

Servings: 1
Counts: 1 Fueling, ½ Lean, 1 Healthy Fat, 1 Green, 1 Condiment

Ingredients:
- 1 tbsp grated Parmesan cheese
- 1 tsp water
- 1 sachet Optavia Essential Roasted Garlic Creamy Smashed Potatoes
- ½ cup reduced fat shredded mozzarella cheese
- 1 cup baby spinach

Directions:
1. Prepare the Roasted Garlic Creamy Smashed Potatoes according to the package directions.
2. Place the spinach in a dish with water and put it in the microwave for one minute.
3. Combine the Roasted Garlic Creamy Smashed Potatoes, mozzarella, spinach, and parmesan cheese in a mixing bowl.

Healthy Margherita Pizza

Servings: 1
Counts: 1 Fueling, ½ Lean, 2 Condiments

Ingredients:
- ¼ cup reduced fat shredded cheese
- 2 tbsp cold water
- 1 sachet Optavia Buttermilk Cheddar Herb Biscuit
- 2 tbsp tomato sauce

Directions:
1. Preheat the oven to 350°F.
2. Mix water and biscuit and place on a circular baking sheet lined with parchment paper. Put it for 10 minutes in the oven.
3. Sprinkle with cheese and tomato sauce and put it in the oven for 5 minutes more, or until the melts completely.

Fresh chocolate and pumpkin cheesecake

Servings: 2
Counts: 1 Fueling, ½ Lean, 1 Healthy Fat, 3 Condiments

Ingredients:
- ½ tbsp butter, melted
- 3 tbsp pumpkin puree
- 3 tbsp light cream cheese
- 2 sachets Optavia Essential Decadent Double Chocolate Brownie
- 2 tbsp cold water
- Pinch salt
- 2 packets zero calorie sugar substitute
- 1 cup reduced fat plain Greek yogurt
- 1 egg
- ½ tsp pumpkin pie spice
- ½ tsp vanilla extract

Directions:
1. Preheat the oven to 350°F.
2. Combine water, butter, and Decadent Double Chocolate Brownie in a mixing bowl. Split the mixture between two mini muffin pans. To make a crust, press the brownie mix into the bottoms of the pans. Put it 15 minutes in the oven.
3. Next, incorporate and combine all of the other ingredients in a mixing bowl until well combined. Split the mixture evenly between the two pans. Reduce the oven temperature to 300°F.
4. Bake for 40 minutes, or until the sides are golden brown and the middle is set. Allow it to cool before removing it from the skillet.

Healthy Chocolate and Coconut Cake

Servings: 2
Counts: 1 Fueling, ½ Lean, 1 Healthy Fat, 1 ½ Condiments

Ingredients:
- 1 Optavia Drizzled Chocolate Fudge Crisp Bar
- 2 tbsp pressurized whipped topping
- 1 sachet Optavia Essential Chocolate Fudge Pudding
- 1 ½ tbsp shredded coconut
- ½ cup coconut milk

Directions:
1. Put the Bar in the microwave for 20 seconds in a serving dish. Fill a small mold halfway with the Bar.
2. Mix milk and Chocolate Fudge Pudding in a mixing bowl. In the ramekin, spread this mix on top of the bar.
3. Refrigerate for about 30 minutes, or until set.
4. Finish with whipped topping.

Tasty Morsels of Cauliflower

Servings: 2
Counts: 1 Fueling, 3 Green, ½ Healthy Fat, 3 Condiments

Ingredients:
- ¼ cup hot buffalo sauce
- ¼ cup reduced fat Greek yogurt
- 2 sachets Optavia Select Buttermilk Cheddar Herb Biscuit
- 1 tsp dry ranch dressing mix
- 3 cups cauliflower florets
- ½ cup water
- ½ tsp butter, melted

Directions:
1. Preheat the oven to 425°F.
2. Mix water and Buttermilk Cheddar Herb Biscuit in a mixing bowl. Continue to mix in the cauliflower until it forms a batter.
3. Bake the cauliflower for 20 minutes on a baking sheet with parchment paper on it.
4. In a separate bowl, incorporate the butter and hot sauce. Mix in the baked cauliflower. Return this mix to the oven for another 10 minutes.
5. Combine the ranch dressing and yogurt in a separate bowl. Serve alongside the cauliflower.

Exotic Coconut Pina Colada

Servings: 1
Counts: ½ Fueling, 3 Condiments

Ingredients:
- 6 oz coconut milk
- ¼ tsp rum extract
- 1 sachet Optavia Essential Creamy Vanilla Shake
- ½ cup ice
- 2 tbsp shredded coconut and 2 tsp for topping
- 6 oz diet ginger ale

Directions:
1. In a food processor or blender combine all of the ingredients and mix until chilly and soft.
2. Pour this into two large glasses and top with the leftover shredded coconut. Enjoy right away!

Fresh Chocolate and Mint Milkshake

Servings: 1
Counts: 1 Fueling, 3 Condiments

Ingredients:
- ½ cup ice
- ¼ tsp peppermint extract
- 1 sachet Optavia Essential Frosty Mint Chocolate Soft Serve Treat
- 4 oz brewed coffee, chilled
- 4 oz vanilla or almond milk
- 2 tbsp pressurized whipped topping
- 2 tbsp sugar free chocolate syrup

Directions:
1. In a high - speed blender, mix and mix milk, water, ice, coffee, peppermint extract, Frosty Mint Chocolate Soft Serve Treat, and one tablespoon chocolate syrup. Merge until the mixture is chilly and soft.
2. Pour into a glass or a plastic cap and garnish with the leftover chocolate syrup and whipped topping.

Bits of Peanut Butter

Servings: 1
Counts: 1 Fueling, 1 Optional Snack

Ingredients:
- 1 Optavia Essential Creamy Double Peanut Butter Crisp Bar
- 1 tbsp water
- 2 tbsp powdered peanut butter

Directions:
1. In a mixing bowl, mix the water and powdered peanut butter to make a smooth dough.
2. Put in the microwave the Creamy Double Peanut Butter Crisp Bar for 15 seconds, or until tender.
3. Create a dough with the peanut butter and the bar.
4. Make four small titbits with your fingers. Place them in the refrigerator and serve cold.

Traditional Mac'n Cheese

Servings: 1
Counts: 1 Fueling, ½ Lean, 3 Condiments

Ingredients:
- ¼ tsp garlic powder
- ½ tbsp tomato paste
- 1 sachet Optavia Cheesy Buttermilk Mac
- ¼ tsp onion powder
- ¼ tsp chili powder
- 3 oz cooked 97% lean ground beef

Directions:
1. Prepare the Cheesy Buttermilk Mac according to the package directions.

2. While the macaroni is still warm, spread and combine in the tomato paste until soft. Continue to mix in the beef and flavourings.

Refreshing Tiramisu Milkshake

Servings: 1
Counts: 1 Fueling, ½ Lean, 2 ½ Condiments

Ingredients:
- 2 tbsp sugar free chocolate syrup
- 2 tbsp pressurized whipped topping
- ½ cup ice
- 1 sachet Optavia Frosty Coffee
- 6 oz plain low-fat Greek yogurt
- ½ cup almond milk

Directions:
1. Combine all of the ingredients in a food processor and puree until soft.
2. Pour into a large glass and top with the whipped topping and syrup.

Gourmet Eggnog

Servings: 1
Counts: 1 Fueling, 1/3 Lean, 1 ½ Condiments

Ingredients:
- ¼ tsp rum extract
- 8 oz vanilla almond milk
- 1 sachet Optavia Essential Creamy Vanilla Shake
- Pinch nutmeg
- 1 pasteurized egg, separated

Directions:
1. In a food processor, combine the Creamy Vanilla Shake, egg yolk, and milk and blend until soft.
2. In a mixing bowl, beat the egg white with a mixer or an electric whisk until it forms a foamy mixture.
3. Pour the shake into a glass with this mix. Season with nutmeg.

Snacks

Celery Sticks with spicy Chicken

Servings: 2
Counts: 1 Healthy Fat, 3 Condiments, ½ Green

Ingredients:
- ¼ tbs each salt and pepper
- ½ cup celery
- 1 tbs mayonnaise
- ¼ cup reduced fat blue cheese dressing
- ¼ cup hot sauce
- 2-6 ounces chicken breast

Directions:
1. Combine mayonnaise and hot sauce in a mixing bowl and garnish with pepper and salt. Mix with the shredded chicken.
2. Stuff celery sticks with the chicken mix.
3. Drizzle with blue cheese dressing.

Counts: 1 Lean, 3 Green

Ingredients:
- 1 cup raw grated cauliflower
- ½ cup Italian diced tomatoes
- ¼ cup egg substitute
- ½ tsp each garlic salt and Italian seasoning
- 1 cup light mozzarella

Healthy Cheese Cauliflower Sticks

Servings: 1

Directions:
1. Preheat the oven to 350°F.
2. Mix 34 cup mozzarella, eggs, and cauliflower in a mixing bowl. Place this mixture on a baking sheet with parchment paper on it. Bake for 30 minutes in the oven. Turn the mix with a spatula and cook for another 15 minutes.
3. Cut the resulting bread into pieces.
4. Top with 14 cup mozzarella, garlic salt, and Italian seasoning to taste.
5. Return the sticks to the oven for another 10 minutes, or until the cheese has melted.

Tortillas with Chicken and Avocado

Servings: 2 (3 tortillas per serving)
Counts: 1 Lean, 2 Green, 1 Healthy Fat, 2 Condiments

Ingredients:
- ¼ tsp pepper
- 3 cauliflower tortillas
- 2 tbs cilantro
- ½ cup eggbeaters
- 1/8 tsp salt
- 2 cups packed cauliflower, grated
- 3 ounces cooked chicken
- 1 ½ ounces avocado
- 1 ounces low fat Mexican cheese, shredded

Directions:
1. Preheat the oven to 375°F for the tortillas.
2. Put in the microwave the cauliflower for 2 minutes on high. Remove a ny extra water and microwave for another 2 minutes.
3. In a mixing bowl, mix the eggs, salt, pepper, and cauliflower. Create 6 circles and arrange them on a baking sheet with parchment paper on it. Bake for 10 minutes, then flip and bake for an additional 7 minutes. Allow them to cool.
4. Combine the cheese, cilantro, chicken, and avocados to make the burrito. 14 of this mix should be added to each tortilla before rolling.
5. Cook the burritos for 2 minutes over moderate flame, then turn and cook for another minute, or until golden brown.

Jalapeno Tiny Boats with Cheddar Cheese

Servings: 2
Counts: 1 Optional Snack, ¼ Lean, 1 Green, 1 Healthy Fat, 2 ½ Condiments

Ingredients:
- 1 sachet Optavia Essential Jalapeno Cheddar Poppers, crushed into breadcrumb
- 2 oz light cream cheese
- ¼ cup low fat Greek yogurt
- ¼ tsp garlic powder
- ¼ tsp chili powder
- ½ cup reduced fat, shredded cheddar jack cheese
- 1/8 tsp salt
- 6 jalapenos, halved lengthwise, membranes and seeds removed

Directions:
1. Preheat the oven to 350°F.
2. Combine Greek yogurt, cheddar jack cheese, cream cheese, garlic powder, chili powder, and salt in a mixing bowl.
3. Fill each jalapeno boat with this mix.
4. Line a baking sheet with parchment and garnish with the Jalapeno Cheddar Poppers.
5. Bake for 20 minutes.

French style Cheese Sticks

Servings: 2 (3 sticks per serving)
Counts: 1 Optional Snack, 3 Condiments

Ingredients:
- 2 sachets Optavia Essential Cinnamon Crunchy O's Cereal
- 6 tbsp liquid egg substitute
- 2 tbsp low fat cream cheese

Directions:
1. Pulse the Cinnamon Crunchy in a food processor or a blender until it resembles breadcrumbs.
2. Stir in the liquid egg substitute and cream cheese until a tender dough is formed.
3. Cut 6 stick pieces from the dough.
4. Cook the sticks in a skillet with oil over moderate flame. Cook until all edges are golden brown.

Popcorn and Cheese Snacks

Servings: 1
Counts: Optional Snack, 3 Condiments

Ingredients:
- 1 tsp grated parmesan cheese
- 1 tsp caramel syrup
- ½ sachet Optavia Puffed Sweet and Salty Snacks
- ½ sachet Optavia Sharp Cheddar and Sour Cream Popcorn

Directions:
1. Mix Sharp Cheddar & Sour Cream Popcorn and Puffed Sweet & Salty Snacks in a mixing bowl. Spread cheese and syrup on top.

Crunchy Zucchini Fries

Servings: 1
Counts: 3 Greens, 1 Healthy Fat, ¼ Condiment

Ingredients:
- 1 ½ cups cooked zucchini
- 1/8 tsp sea salt
- 1 tsp olive oil

Directions:
1. Preheat the oven to 200°F.
2. Line a parchment paper-covered baking sheet and arrange the zucchini slices on it. Sprinkle them with olive oil.
3. Bake for 3 hours, or until the zucchini slices are crispy.

Crispy Fish Sticks

Servings: 4
Counts: 1 Lean, 2 Healthy Fat, 3 Green, 2 Condiments
Nutrition: 390 Calories, 47g Protein, 17g Carbohydrate, 15g Fat

Ingredients:

- 6 tbsp almond flour
- 6 cups green beans, trimmed
- ¼ tsp ground black pepper
- ¼ tsp salt
- 2 tbsp parmesan cheese
- 6 tbsp mayonnaise
- ½ cup basil, chopped
- 2 lbs cod fillets, sliced into 16 sticks
- 1 clove garlic, minced

Directions:

1. Preheat the oven to 425°F.
2. Mix salt, pepper, parmesan, and almond flour in a mixing bowl.
3. Apply this mix to both sides of the fish.
4. Place them on a baking sheet covered with parchment paper and bake for 6 minutes, or until roasted.
5. Finally, bring a pot of water to a boil and cook the green beans. Cook for 4 minutes, or until crunchy.
6. To make the garlic and basil sauce, combine the basil, garlic, and mayonnaise in a mixing bowl.
7. Top each serving with 4 fish sticks, 1 tbsp basil sauce, and 12 cup green beans.

Honey chicken nuggets

Servings: 2
Counts: 1 Lean, 2 Condiments

Ingredients:

- 1 egg, beaten
- 12 oz skinless, boneless chicken breast, cubed
- ¼ cup reduced fat Greek yogurt
- 2 sachets Optavia Essential Honey Mustard & Onion Sticks, crushed into breadcrumb
- ¼ tsp garlic powder
- 2 tsp spicy brown mustard

Directions:

1. Preheat the oven to 400°F.
2. Separate the egg and the Honey Mustard & Onion Sticks into two bowls. Each chicken piece should be dipped in the egg and then rolled in the Honey Mustard. Place the chicken pieces on a baking sheet covered with parchment paper and bake for 20 minutes, or until the outside is golden brown and the inner temperature has reached 165°F.
3. In a separate bowl, combine the mustard, garlic powder, and Greek yogurt. With this yogurt seasoning, serve the nuggets.

Tiny Vegetable Omelettes

Servings: 4
Counts: 1 Lean, 3 Green, 3 Condiments
Nutrition: 290 Calories, 25g Protein, 10g Carbohydrate, 17g Fat

Ingredients:
- 2 cups quartered mushrooms
- 2 cups small broccoli florets
- 2 cups diced red bell peppers
- ¼ tsp salt
- ¼ tsp ground black pepper
- 2 oz reduced fat, crumbled feta

Directions:
1. Preheat the oven to 400°F.
2. Combine the eggs with salt and pepper in a sheet pan lined with parchment paper.
3. Top the beaten eggs with broccoli florets, mushrooms, red bell peppers, and feta.
4. Bake for 15 minutes, or until the omelettes are done.
5. Remove from oven and divide into four equal portions.

Original Pumpkin Popcorn Snack

Servings: 1
Counts: 1 Optional Snack, 3 Condiments

Ingredients:
- ½ tsp pumpkin seed kernels
- ¼ tsp pumpkin pie spice
- 1 sachet Optavia Olive Oil & Sea Salt Popcorn
- 1/3 tbsp pancake syrup
- ½ tbsp slivered almonds

Directions:
1. Mix pumpkin pie spice and syrup in a mixing bowl.
2. In a mixing bowl, combine the Olive Oil & Sea Salt Popcorn, pumpkin seed kernels, and slivered almonds. Pour over the syrup mixture.
3. Distribute uniformly on the popcorn.

Special Cheeseburger Pie

Servings: 4
Counts: 1 Lean, 3 Green, 3 Condiments, ½ Optional Snack
Nutrition: 310 Calories, 35g Protein, 15 Carbohydrate, 13g Fat

Ingredients:
- 1 large spaghetti squash
- 2 tbsp tomato paste
- ½ tsp Worcestershire sauce
- 1lb 94% lean ground beef
- 2 eggs
- 2 oz dill pickle slices
- 2/3 cup reduced fat, shredded cheddar cheese
- ¼ cup diced onion
- 1/3 cup low fat Greek yogurt

Directions:
1. Preheat the oven to 400°F.
2. Cut the spaghetti squash in half lengthwise and scoop out the pulp and seeds. Bake for 30 minutes with the spaghetti halves cut side down on a baking sheet lined with parchment paper. Allow to cool after cooking.
3. Scrape the squash flesh to eliminate any remaining strands.
4. Prepare 6 cups spaghetti squash and save the rest for other recipes. Make a layer of squash strands at the pan's end and sides.
5. For the pie filling, brown the beef and onion in a skillet with oil over medium heat for 10 minutes, or until the beef is brow. Take the pan off the heat.
6. Mix Greek yogurt, tomato paste, eggs, and Worcestershire sauce in a mixing bowl. Add the ground beef and mix well. Place all of this on top of the squash crust. Spread cheese and dill pickle slices on top of the meat filling.
7. Cook for 40 minutes. Then, divide the mixture into four equal portions and serve.

Spicy Burrito with Spinach

Servings: 2
Counts: 1 Lean, 3 Green, 3 Condiments, 1 Healthy Fat
Nutrition: 350 Calories, 29g Protein, 19g Carbohydrate, 17g Fat

Ingredients:
- 1 cup shredded, reduced fat pepper jack cheese
- ¼ cup cilantro, chopped
- 1 jalapeno pepper, diced
- 1 cup diced tomatoes
- 4 eggs whites
- 2 eggs
- 2 tsp balsamic vinegar
- 1 tbsp red onion, chopped
- 2 tbsp whole flax seeds
- 2 cups baby spinach, chopped
- 1 clove garlic, minced
- 1/8 tsp each salt and pepper
- ½ cup diced bell pepper

Directions:
1. To make the tortilla, combine the first three ingredients in a bowl.
2. Cook the half egg mixture in a pan with oil over moderate flame. Spread them evenly across the skillet to form a tortilla. Cook for another two minutes. Cook until the eggs are fully set, then flip. Repeat the procedure with the remaining half of the egg mixture.
3. Sauté the spinach for about 3 minutes in the same skillet.
4. Combine all of the salsa ingredients in a mixing bowl.
5. Put a tortilla on a plate, top with half of the spinach, salsa, and cheese, and wrap up to make a burrito.

Tidbits of Mushrooms with Cheese

Servings: 2
Counts: 1 Lean, 3 Green, 2 Condiments

Ingredients:
- ½ tsp Italian seasoning
- 2 cups reduced fat shredded mozzarella cheese
- 1 tbsp lemon juice
- 4 large mushroom caps, stemmed
- ½ cup chopped tomato
- 1 tbsp soy sauce
- 1 tsp olive oil
- 1 tbsp chopped cilantro
- 1 clove garlic, minced

Directions:
1. Preheat the oven to 400°F.
2. Eliminate the inner caps of the mushrooms with a spoon to make bowls.
3. Combine soy sauce, lemon juice, and half of the olive oil in a mixing bowl. Bake this mix for 12 minutes on a baking tray lined with parchment paper.
4. Mix the tomatoes, Italian seasoning, mozzarella, garlic, and the remaining olive oil in a separate bowl.
5. Place the mixture into the mushroom caps and bake for 7 minutes, or until the cheese melts.
6. Garnish with fresh cilantro.

Tiny Cauliflower Rolls

Servings: 4 (3 rolls per serving)
Counts: ½ Lean, 2 Green, 3 Condiments

Ingredients:
- 2 tbsp fresh rosemary, chopped
- ½ tsp salt
- 4 cup riced cauliflower
- 1/3 cup reduced fat mozzarella cheese, or cheddar cheese
- 2 eggs
- 1/3 cup almond flour

Directions:
1. Preheat the oven to 400°F.
2. Combine all of the ingredients in a mixing bowl. In a baking sheet lined with parchment paper, divide the cauliflower mixture equally into 12 rolls.
3. Bake for 30 minutes, or until the top is golden brown.

Mini Cauliflower Pancakes

Servings: 2
Counts: ½ Lean, 3 Green, 3 Condiments, 1 Optional Snack

Ingredients:
- ½ cup sliced green onion
- 1 egg
- 2 sachets Rosemary Sea Salt Crackers, ground to a flour consistency
- 1 cup reduced fat Greek yogurt
- ¼ tsp each salt and pepper
- ¼ cup diced yellow onion
- 2 ½ cup riced cauliflower

Directions:
1. In a mixing bowl, combine all of the ingredients except the Greek yogurt and green onion.
2. Warm the oil in a skillet over medium heat. Then, split one-third of the cauliflower mix between two mounds on the skillet.
3. Compress them so that they have a circular form. Cook for 5 minutes on each side, or until golden brown. Repeat with the rest of the mix.
4. Season with green onion and Greek yogurt.

Mini Mushroom Italian Pizza

Servings: 1
Counts: 1 Lean, 3 Green, 3 Condiments

Ingredients:
- 2.2 oz mushrooms caps, stems removed
- 4. Oz reduced fat shredded mozzarella cheese
- ¼ cup Italian tomato sauce

Directions:
1. Line a parchment paper-covered baking sheet and put the mushroom caps on top. Bake for 10 minutes, or until the potatoes are soft.
2. Spread tomato sauce equally on each cap, then top with cheese. Bake for another 4 minutes, or until the cheese has melted.

Gourmet Cauliflower Pizza Snack

Servings: 2
Counts: 1 Lean, 3 Green, 3 Condiments

Ingredients:
- 1 tbsp diced red onion
- ¼ small green bell pepper, diced
- 3 tbsp parmesan cheese
- 2 eggs
- 2 ½ cups riced cauliflower
- ½ tsp Italian seasoning
- 1/8 tsp salt
- 1 tbsp sliced black olives
- 6 turkey pepperoni slices, chopped
- 1 ¼ cup reduced fat shredded mozzarella cheese, divided
- ¼ cup tomato sauce

Directions:
1. Preheat the oven to 400°F.
2. Place the riced cauliflower in a bowl and put in the microwave for 10 minutes.
3. Allow to cool before adding the parmesan, Italian seasoning, eggs, 14 cup mozzarella, and salt.
4. Spoon this mix into the 12 muffin pan slots. Bake for 20 minutes with a light press to form small crusts.
5. Spread tomato sauce on top of each cauliflower crust. Pepperoni, bell peppers, cheese, onion, and olives are all options. Bake for 7 minutes, or until the cheese melts.

Fresh and fast Shrimp Salad

Servings: 1
Counts: 1 Lean, 3 Green, 1 Healthy Fat, 1 Optional Snack

Ingredients:
- ½ cup cherry tomatoes, halved
- 1 slice turkey bacon, chopped
- 1 sachet Optavia Puffed Ranch Snack
- 1 tbsp ranch dressing
- 2 cups romaine lettuce
- 4 oz cooked and peeled shrimp
- 1/8 avocado, diced
- 1 hard-boiled egg, sliced

Directions:
1. Combine the shrimp, tomatoes, eggs, lettuce, avocado, and turkey bacon in a mixing bowl.
2. Garnish with Puffed Ranch Snacks and ranch dressing and serve right away.

Spicy Jicama Snack

Servings: 2
Counts: 3 Green, 1 ½ Condiment, ½ Healthy Fat

Ingredients:
<ul><li>½ tsp onion powder</li><li>1 tsp paprika</li><li>1 medium sized jicama, cut into fries, 3 cups</li><li>½ tsp each salt and pepper</li><li>1 tsp olive oil</li></ul>

Directions:

1. Preheat the oven to 400°F.
2. Peel the jicama skin off with a knife or potato peeler. Trim the jicama into thin slices, similar to how you would cut fries.
3. Toss the jicama fries with the paprika, onion powder, olive oil, salt, and pepper in a mixing bowl.
4. Place them on a baking sheet covered with parchment paper and bake for 30 minutes.

Meal plan 5&1

	Week 1	Week 2
Monday	Pizza Muffins Traditional Mac'n Cheese Healthy Margherita Pizza Sweet Pumpkin Milkshake Fresh Chocolate and Mint Milkshake Tasty chicken and cheese	Waffles topped with potatoes and melted cheese Bits of Peanut Butter Exotic Coconut Pina Colada Fun Colorful Frappe Gourmet Eggnog Grated spaghetti squash
Tuesday	Cream cheese and berry donut Biscuits with Greek yogurt and chocolate Fun Colorful Frappe Pizza Muffins Bagel with Cheddar Cheese Healthy Salmon Salad	Traditional Mac'n Cheese Gourmet Eggnog Sweet Pumpkin Milkshake Chocolate and Peanut Butter Donuts Fresh Chocolate and Mint Milkshake Fresh salmon with a salad of tomatoes and cucumbers
Wednesday	Sweet Pumpkin Milkshake Bagel with Cheddar Cheese Cream cheese and berry donut Fresh Chocolate and Mint Milkshake Chocolate and Peanut Butter Donuts Pie Made with Cauliflower and Melted Cheese	Fresh chocolate and pumpkin cheesecake Waffles topped with potatoes and melted cheese Gourmet Eggnog Pizza Muffins Fun Colorful Frappe Shrimp and Oriental Cauliflower Rice
Thursday	Tasty Morsels of Cauliflower Healthy Chocolate and Coconut Cake Waffles topped with potatoes and melted cheese Pizza Muffins Greedy Avocado Toast Risotto of Cauliflower and Asparagus with Chicken	Gourmet Eggnog Fresh chocolate and pumpkin cheesecake Sweet Pumpkin Milkshake Goat cheese muffins Healthy Margherita Pizza Mexican Pork Stew
	Healthy Chocolate and Coconut Cake	Goat cheese muffins

Friday	Biscuits with Greek yogurt and chocolate	Exotic Coconut Pina Colada
	Greedy Avocado Toast	Traditional Mac'n Cheese
	Fresh chocolate and pumpkin cheesecake	Fresh Chocolate and Mint Milkshake
	Gourmet Eggnog	Healthy Margherita Pizza
	Traditional Korean Bibimbap	Chicken with fresh and healthy Vegetables
Saturday	Bits of Peanut Butter	Fun Colorful Frappe
	Biscuits with Greek yogurt and chocolate	Italian style Marinara Rigatoni
	Traditional Mac'n Cheese	Greedy Avocado Toast
	Creamy Potatoes with Spinach and Cheese	Tasty Morsels of Cauliflower
	Bagel with Cheddar Cheese	Healthy Margherita Pizza
	Exotic Chicken	Spaghetti squash with Bolognese sauce
Sunday	Pizza Muffins	Cream cheese and berry donut
	Creamy Potatoes with Spinach and Cheese	Healthy Margherita Pizza
	Greedy Avocado Toast	Exotic Coconut Pina Colada
	Bagel with Cheddar Cheese	Traditional Mac'n Cheese
	Chocolate and Peanut Butter Donuts	Fresh Chocolate and Mint Milkshake
	Mediterranean style chicken	Chicken with an Asian twist

	Week 3	Week 4
Monday	Healthy Chocolate and Coconut Cake	Cream cheese and berry donut
	Chocolate and Peanut Butter Donuts	Goat cheese muffins
	Fresh chocolate and pumpkin cheesecake	Greedy Avocado Toast
	Creamy Potatoes with Spinach and Cheese	Tasty Morsels of Cauliflower
	Italian style Marinara Rigatoni	Biscuits with Greek yogurt and chocolate
	Manicotti with spinach and zucchini	Delicious lasagna with vegetables
Tuesday	Fresh chocolate and pumpkin cheesecake	Waffles topped with potatoes and melted cheese
	Tasty Morsels of Cauliflower	Healthy Chocolate and Coconut Cake
	Goat cheese muffins	Bits of Peanut Butter
	Italian style Marinara Rigatoni	Greedy Avocado Toast
	Creamy Potatoes with Spinach and Cheese	Healthy Margherita Pizza

	Mushroom Boats with taco filling	Eggplant Filled with Shrimp and Cauliflower
Wednesday	Goat cheese muffins	Italian style Marinara Rigatoni
	Bits of Peanut Butter	Exotic Coconut Pina Colada
	Creamy Potatoes with Spinach and Cheese	Tasty Morsels of Cauliflower
	Traditional Mac'n Cheese	Biscuits with Greek yogurt and chocolate
	Healthy Chocolate and Coconut Cake	Greedy Avocado Toast
	Tasty Chicken Paella	Mouthwatering Chicken with Asparagus
Thursday	Fun Colorful Frappe	Bagel with Cheddar Cheese
	Traditional Mac'n Cheese	Italian style Marinara Rigatoni
	Cream cheese and berry donut	Creamy Potatoes with Spinach and Cheese
	Biscuits with Greek yogurt and chocolate	Fresh Chocolate and Mint Milkshake
	Chocolate and Peanut Butter Donuts	Bits of Peanut Butter
	Greek style Cod	Hispanic flavored turkey
Friday	Pizza Muffins	Chocolate and Peanut Butter Donuts
	Creamy Potatoes with Spinach and Cheese	Sweet Pumpkin Milkshake
	Bagel with Cheddar Cheese	Fun Colorful Frappe
	Cream cheese and berry donut	Waffles topped with potatoes and melted cheese
	Bits of Peanut Butter	Tasty Morsels of Cauliflower
	Seafood with vegetables	Pepperoni Italian pizza
Saturday	Fresh chocolate and pumpkin cheesecake	Chocolate and Peanut Butter Donuts
	Waffles topped with potatoes and melted cheese	Exotic Coconut Pina Colada
	Sweet Pumpkin Milkshake	Fresh Chocolate and Mint Milkshake
	Healthy Chocolate and Coconut Cake	Pizza Muffins
	Gourmet Eggnog	Cream cheese and berry donut
	Salmon filet with Vegetables	Creamy asparagus and crabmeat omelette
Sunday	Tasty Morsels of Cauliflower	Bits of Peanut Butter
	Italian style Marinara Rigatoni	Fun Colorful Frappe
	Gourmet Eggnog	Sweet Pumpkin Milkshake

Biscuits with Greek yogurt and chocolate	Waffles topped with potatoes and melted cheese
Fresh chocolate and pumpkin cheesecake	
	Goat cheese muffins
Pizza with cauliflower crust and chicken	Mexican Fajita

Meal plan 4&2&1

	Week 1	Week 2
Monday	Bits of Peanut Butter	Goat cheese muffins
	Fun Colorful Frappe	Tasty Morsels of Cauliflower
	Sweet Pumpkin Milkshake	Italian style Marinara Rigatoni
	Waffles topped with potatoes and melted cheese	Gourmet Eggnog
	Tasty chicken and cheese	Delicious lasagna with vegetables
	Grated spaghetti squash	Healthy Salmon Salad
		Fresh salmon with a salad of tomatoes and cucumbers
	Manicotti with spinach and zucchini	
Tuesday	Creamy Potatoes with Spinach and Cheese	Greedy Avocado Toast
		Creamy Potatoes with Spinach and Cheese
	Greedy Avocado Toast	
	Bagel with Cheddar Cheese	Healthy Margherita Pizza
	Chocolate and Peanut Butter Donuts	Bits of Peanut Butter
	Risotto of Cauliflower and Asparagus with Chicken	Hispanic flavored turkey
	Mexican Pork Stew	Pepperoni Italian pizza
	Greek style Cod	Seafood with vegetables
Wednesday	Sweet Pumpkin Milkshake	Tasty Morsels of Cauliflower
	Fresh Chocolate and Mint Milkshake	Exotic Coconut Pina Colada
	Goat cheese muffins	Pizza Muffins
	Cream cheese and berry donut	Biscuits with Greek yogurt and chocolate
	Mexican Fajita	Mediterranean style chicken
	Pizza with cauliflower crust and chicken	Tacos with cheddar cheese and avocado
		Chicken with Broccoli with Japanese flavors
	Chicken with an Asian twist	

Thursday	Gourmet Eggnog	Exotic Coconut Pina Colada
	Goat cheese muffins	Fresh chocolate and pumpkin cheesecake
	Creamy Potatoes with Spinach and Cheese	Fresh Chocolate and Mint Milkshake
	Chocolate and Peanut Butter Donuts	Tasty Morsels of Cauliflower
	Delicious Buffalo Chicken dip with Vegan Chips	Tasty chicken and cheese
	Oriental Chicken Tikka Masala	Grated spaghetti squash
	Healthy Chicken with Kohlrabi Noodle	Manicotti with spinach and zucchini
Friday	Sweet Pumpkin Milkshake	Exotic Coconut Pina Colada
	Healthy Chocolate and Coconut Cake	Waffles topped with potatoes and melted cheese
	Pizza Muffins	Healthy Margherita Pizza
	Bagel with Cheddar Cheese	Greedy Avocado Toast
	Shrimp and Oriental Cauliflower Rice	Risotto of Cauliflower and Asparagus with Chicken
	Tasty Chicken Paella	Mexican Pork Stew
	Mouthwatering Chicken with Asparagus	Greek style Cod
Saturday	Fresh Chocolate and Mint Milkshake	Creamy Potatoes with Spinach and Cheese
	Biscuits with Greek yogurt and chocolate	
	Waffles topped with potatoes and melted cheese	Bagel with Cheddar Cheese
		Cream cheese and berry donut
	Bits of Peanut Butter	Fresh chocolate and pumpkin cheesecake
	Salmon filet with Vegetables	Mexican Fajita
	Spaghetti squash with Bolognese sauce	Pizza with cauliflower crust and chicken
	Exotic Chicken	Chicken with an Asian twist
Sunday	Goat cheese muffins	Cream cheese and berry donut
	Waffles topped with potatoes and melted cheese	Italian style Marinara Rigatoni
	Bagel with Cheddar Cheese	Pizza Muffins
	Bits of Peanut Butter	Exotic Coconut Pina Colada
		Delicious Buffalo Chicken dip with Vegan Chips
	Japanese-style beef	
	Chinese Chicken	Oriental Chicken Tikka Masala
	Traditional Shakshuka	Healthy Chicken with Kohlrabi Noodle

	Week 3	Week 4
Monday	Biscuits with Greek yogurt and chocolate	Exotic Coconut Pina Colada
	Fresh chocolate and pumpkin cheesecake	Traditional Mac'n Cheese
	Cream cheese and berry donut	Fresh Chocolate and Mint Milkshake
	Healthy Margherita Pizza	Pizza Muffins
	Mushroom Boats with taco filling	Shrimp and Oriental Cauliflower Rice
	Eggplant Filled with Shrimp and Cauliflower	Tasty Chicken Paella
	Pie Made with Cauliflower and Melted Cheese	Mouthwatering Chicken with Asparagus
Tuesday	Fresh chocolate and pumpkin cheesecake	Waffles topped with potatoes and melted cheese
	Gourmet Eggnog	Traditional Mac'n Cheese
	Bagel with Cheddar Cheese	Italian style Marinara Rigatoni
	Healthy Chocolate and Coconut Cake	Chocolate and Peanut Butter Donuts
	Chicken with fresh and healthy Vegetables	Salmon filet with Vegetables
	Traditional Korean Bibimbap	Spaghetti squash with Bolognese sauce
	Creamy asparagus and crabmeat omelette	Exotic Chicken
Wednesday	Fun Colorful Frappe	Sweet Pumpkin Milkshake
	Bits of Peanut Butter	Greedy Avocado Toast
	Cream cheese and berry donut	Pizza Muffins
	Traditional Mac'n Cheese	Healthy Margherita Pizza
	Mexican Meatloaf	Japanese-style beef
	Salmon with Asparagus	Chinese Chicken
	Asian Chicken with Noodles	Traditional Shakshuka
Thursday	Italian style Marinara Rigatoni	Fresh chocolate and pumpkin cheesecake
	Biscuits with Greek yogurt and chocolate	Creamy Potatoes with Spinach and Cheese
	Waffles topped with potatoes and melted cheese	Fresh Chocolate and Mint Milkshake
	Healthy Chocolate and Coconut Cake	Bits of Peanut Butter
	Delicious lasagna with vegetables	Mushroom Boats with taco filling
	Healthy Salmon Salad	Eggplant Filled with Shrimp and Cauliflower

Fresh salmon with a salad of tomatoes and cucumbers	Pie Made with Cauliflower and Melted Cheese

Friday	Gourmet Eggnog Cream cheese and berry donut Traditional Mac'n Cheese Tasty Morsels of Cauliflower Hispanic flavored turkey Pepperoni Italian pizza Seafood with vegetables	Biscuits with Greek yogurt and chocolate Fun Colorful Frappe Italian style Marinara Rigatoni Goat cheese muffins Chicken with fresh and healthy Vegetables Traditional Korean Bibimbap Creamy asparagus and crabmeat omelette
Saturday	Exotic Coconut Pina Colada Goat cheese muffins Healthy Chocolate and Coconut Cake Healthy Margherita Pizza Mediterranean style chicken Tacos with cheddar cheese and avocado Chicken with Broccoli with Japanese flavors	Sweet Pumpkin Milkshake Greedy Avocado Toast Gourmet Eggnog Fun Colorful Frappe Mexican Meatloaf Salmon with Asparagus Asian Chicken with Noodles
Sunday	Tasty Morsels of Cauliflower Fun Colorful Frappe Sweet Pumpkin Milkshake Healthy Margherita Pizza Tasty chicken and cheese Grated spaghetti squash Manicotti with spinach and zucchini	Italian style Marinara Rigatoni Pizza Muffins Traditional Mac'n Cheese Tasty Morsels of Cauliflower Delicious lasagna with vegetables Healthy Salmon Salad Fresh salmon with a salad of tomatoes and cucumbers

Conclusion

Here we are at the end of this guide, which I hope has given you the power to begin your new life and your new healthy food journey while also providing you with a variety of intriguing and yummy recipes. As we've seen, I have made room for a variety of ingredients that will be included in your new nutritional plan. You are guided step by step from breakfast to dinner. In fact, each recipe contains the accurate number of calories, proteins, carbohydrates, and fats, allowing you to adjust them day after day and plan your meals accordingly. My goal was to develop recipe ideas that I would use and try to replicate at home and then share them with you. It would have been a real pity not to spread them and assist others who, like me, have decided to change their way of life and feel much better every day. In fact, the lean and green diet has been proven scientifically to prevent heart disease and other physical and psychological ailments. As a result, you will benefit from it in the long run.

It is a diet with many advantages, and you will notice that the foods mentioned in the recipes are not pricey. Fruits and vegetables, as well as tofu and meat, are frequently inexpensive.

It's also a very trendy diet. Many actors and musicians have been following it for some time and have discovered many benefits.

Frappé or snacks are frequently preferred components of this diet. They are fast and simple to prepare, and most importantly, they are delicious. They can be appreciated at home while sitting comfortably on the sofa, or at work as a nice break. I'm sure your friends and coworkers will be curious about your new dishes and want to know what they are.

My coworkers were fascinated by the meals I brought to work, and they began to replicate them as well. Even now, they thank me for helping them lose weight and feel more energized.

They have seen positive changes in both their personal and work lives. Their productivity has risen, and some of them have been promoted at work. This enables you to comprehend how the lean and green diet is sincerely a diet revolution. You will not have to give up your favorite dishes, but they will be rebuilt to be healthier and more nutritious.

As a result, I am confident that this manual will help you achieve your dietary goals and finally begin this new and thrilling adventure.

Thanks for reading!